W9-CHZ-725

TECHNOLOGY IN ANCIENT CULTURES

ANCIENT MACHINE TECHNOLOGY

FROM WHEELS TO FORGES

Michael Woods and
Mary B. Woods

Twenty-First Century Books · Minneapolis

To school librarians, teachers, moms, dads, and others who help kids read

Twenty-First Century Books
A division of Lerner Publishing Group, Inc.
241 First Avenue North
Minneapolis, MN 55401 U.S.A.

Website address: www.lernerbooks.com

Library of Congress Cataloging-in-Publication Data

Woods, Michael, 1946–
    Ancient machine technology : from wheels to forges / Michael Woods and Mary B. Woods.
        p. cm. — (Technology in ancient cultures)
    Includes bibliographical references and index.
    ISBN 978-0-7613-6523-5 (lib. bdg. : alk. paper)
        1. Wedges—History—to 1500—Juvenile literature. 2. Wheels—History—to 1500—Juvenile literature. I. Woods, Mary B. (Mary Boyle), 1946– II. Title.
    TJ1201.W44W66 2011
    621.8093—dc22   2010025583

Manufactured in the United States of America
1 – PC – 12/31/10

TABLE OF CONTENTS

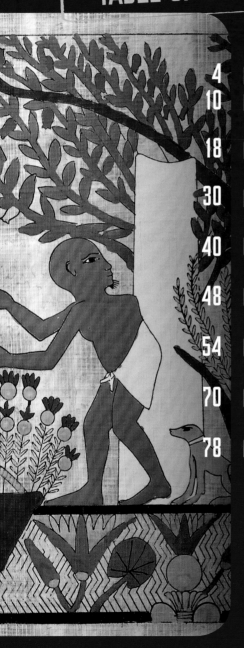

THE ANCIENT WORLDS OF MACHINES

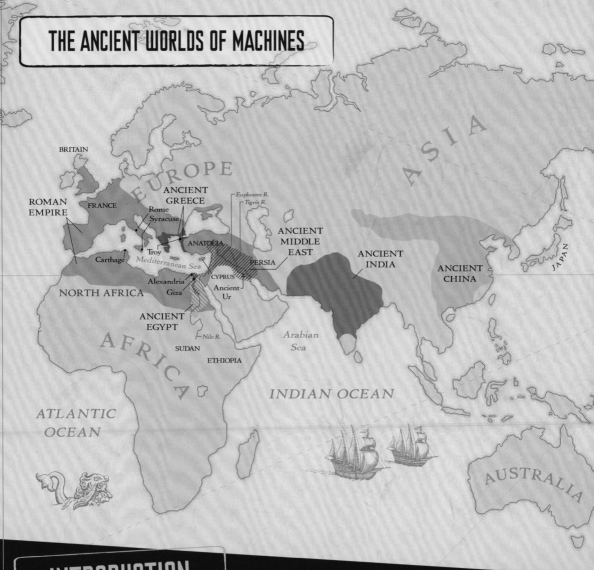

INTRODUCTION

What do you think of when you hear the word *technology*? You probably think of something totally new. You might think of research laboratories filled with computers, powerful microscopes, and other scientific tools. But technology doesn't refer only to brand-new machines and discoveries. Technology is as old as human society.

GREENLAND

ARCTIC

NORTH AMERICA

N

PACIFIC OCEAN

ATLANTIC OCEAN

MESOAMERICA

CENTRAL AMERICA

SOUTH AMERICA

PERU

BOLIVIA

INCA EMPIRE

Andes Mountains

- ANCIENT INDIA
- ROMAN EMPIRE
- ANCIENT GREECE
- MESOAMERICA
- ANCIENT CHINA
- ANCIENT EGYPT
- ANCIENT MIDDLE EAST
- INCA EMPIRE
- ♣ Ancient Site
- • City
- ⌂ Mountains

Technology is the use of knowledge, inventions, and discoveries to make human life better. The word *technology* comes from two Greek words. One, *techne*, means "art" or "craft." The other, *logia*, means "reason" or "logic." The ancient Greeks originally used the word *technology* to mean a discussion of arts and crafts. In modern times, *technology* usually refers to a craft, a technique, or a tool itself.

People use many kinds of technology. Medicine is one kind of technology. Transportation and agriculture are also kinds of technologies. These technologies and many others help make human life easier, safer, and more enjoyable. This book looks at another important kind of technology, one that has helped human life tremendously. That technology is machinery.

ON THE JOB

A machine is a device that does work. You know what work means. Work usually involves doing or making something—accomplishing a task. But engineers have a special definition of work. To engineers, work means transferring energy from one object to another. This transfer of energy causes the object to move or change direction. When an engine moves a car, the engine is doing work. When you turn the pages of this book, you are doing work. The amount of work depends on the amount of force applied to the object and the distance the object moves. Force means push or pull.

Machines allow people to apply more force and do more work than could be done with muscle power alone. With machines, people can also apply force more efficiently.

Some machines have hundreds of moving parts. They get their power from motors. Other machines are very basic. For example, scissors, tweezers, knives, and bottle openers are not

▶ These bronze ax heads from 1800 B.C. were found in modern-day Iran. They are examples of wedges, one of six simple machines.

complicated. They do not have ball bearings, pistons, gears, or valves. They do not burn fuel. They are easy to use. Yet they are machines.

LEARNING FROM THE PAST

Archaeologists are scientists who study the remains of past cultures. Sometimes it's easy for archaeologists to learn about ancient machines. If the machines were built out of stone or metal, they might still exist. Archaeologists can find and study them. If the machines were made of wood, animal hide, or plant fibers, they might have rotted away long ago. But archaeologists can still learn about these machines. Sometimes ancient people drew pictures or wrote descriptions of machines.

▲ This relief image, created around 2325 B.C., is from a tomb in the ancient Egyptian burial grounds of Saqqara. It shows two sculptors using hammers and chisels to carve a statue. Many ancient cultures depicted machines and tools in their artwork.

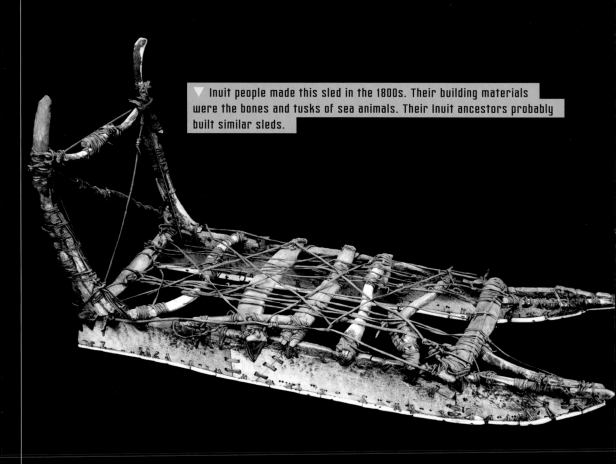

▼ Inuit people made this sled in the 1800s. Their building materials were the bones and tusks of sea animals. Their Inuit ancestors probably built similar sleds.

Often people made the same kinds of machines year after year, for thousands of years. So if archaeologists wanted to know what Australian boomerangs looked like ten thousand years ago, they might examine boomerangs made just a few hundred years ago. The ancient boomerangs and the newer ones would be very similar.

In modern times, engineers have improved on ancient ideas. They have developed oils to make machines with moving parts work more efficiently. They have learned to make machines faster, more precise, more powerful, and more durable. But some ancient machines haven't changed much. For instance, if you've ever used a wheelbarrow, you were using technology developed in China more than two thousand years ago.

SIMPLE AND COMPLEX

All machines, no matter how complicated they seem, are based on some combination of six "simple machines." The simple machines are the lever, the wheel and axle, the inclined plane, the pulley, the wedge, and the screw. Ancient people used all six simple machines. They also combined different kinds of simple machines to create more complex ones.

In this book, you'll learn about the simple machines and the complicated ones. The simple machines include axes for cutting wood and knives for butchering meat. The complicated machines include the Claws of Archimedes. This device from ancient Greece could lift whole battleships out of the water and smash them to pieces. What other machines did ancient people use? Read on to find out.

CHAPTER ONE

MACHINE BASICS

The first humans on Earth lived about 2.5 million years ago. They were hunters and gatherers. They lived in small groups. They got their food by hunting game, fishing, and gathering wild plants. When the food in one area was all used up, the group moved to a new place.

In some places on Earth, the hunter-gatherer lifestyle remained unchanged until only a few centuries ago. In other places, people gradually gave up hunting and gathering and became herders, farmers, and city dwellers.

SIMPLE MACHINE: THE LEVER

Hunter-gatherers made tools from stone, wood, animal bones, animal hides, plant fibers, and clay. One of these tools was the lever, one of the six simple machines. A lever is a bar or beam used to lift objects or pry them loose. Hunter-gatherers used sticks to pry big rocks from the ground. They also used sticks to pry edible roots from the ground. These sticks were levers.

When you push down on one end of a lever, the other end can lift a load, such as a rock stuck in the ground. The lever pivots, or turns, on a support called a fulcrum. The first fulcrum was probably the ground itself. But early peoples probably realized that using a rock or a piece of wood as a fulcrum made prying easier.

Oars and paddles are types of levers. Think of an ancient fisher paddling a boat on a lake. The paddle handle is one end of a lever. The side of the boat acts as a fulcrum. The blade of the paddle is the other end of the lever. The person paddling supplies the force in the form of muscle power. The moving blade pushes on the water, propelling the boat across the lake.

A modern Australian man shows how to use a spear thrower. The end of the spear sits in the thrower. When the man brings his arm forward, the spear shoots from the thrower with extra power and speed.

A craftsperson in ancient France carved this spear thrower thirteen thousand years ago. The tool is made of reindeer bone.

A spear thrower is another kind of lever. Ancient people around the world used spear throwers to help them throw spears farther. The front end of the spear thrower rested in a hunter's hand, along with the spear. When the hunter released the spear, the back end of the spear thrower pushed the spear forward with extra force. With a spear thrower, a human hunter could propel a spear four times farther than could be done with muscle power alone. The oldest known spear throwers come from caves in France. They date from 15,000 to 11,000 B.C. We know that ancient Australians used spear throwers because they are pictured in many rock carvings in Australia. In North America, spear throwers were called atlatls. Ancient peoples mostly made spear throwers out of wood. Sometimes they used antlers or another natural material to make spear throwers.

WHICH WOOD?

Early peoples got all their tools and supplies from the natural world. The forests provided a range of different woods. The choice of wood depended on what a craftsperson wanted to make.

Wood	Qualities	Good for Making
Willow	Bends easily	Baskets
Cedar	Doesn't rot quickly, even in water	Boats
Hickory and ash	Don't split easily	Tool handles
Oak	Extremely strong	Levers, wedges

SIMPLE MACHINE: THE WEDGE

Early peoples used another simple machine, the wedge. A wedge is a piece of wood, stone, metal, or other material that is thicker at one end than at the other. Needles, knives, axes, and chisels are all wedges. Our front teeth even work as wedges.

People can use wedges to move loads a short distance. Imagine cutting an apple with a knife. The tip of the knife, the thinnest edge, begins to split the apple. As the knife moves deeper into the apple, the wider edge splits the apple even more.

This knife was made in Egypt more than five thousand years ago. The handle is ivory, and the wedge-shaped knife blade is a hard stone called flint.

Early peoples made many wedges out of stone. These included stone axes, knives, scrapers, and arrowheads. People made these tools by knapping, or knocking, two stones together. By carefully directing their blows, they were able to create tools with razor-sharp edges.

Flint was the best stone for toolmaking. Flint is a hard stone, but it breaks apart evenly and cleanly. A skilled ancient knapper could chip away at the edges of a piece of flint to create a smooth, sharp blade. The tool would have been sharp enough to butcher mammoths and other large animals that ancient peoples hunted for food.

TOP TOOLMAKERS

Early humans called Cro-Magnons were skilled toolmakers. They lived in Europe between thirty-five thousand and ten thousand years ago. Cro-Magnon craftspeople carved stone, animal bones, and animal horns into precision tools. These tools include harpoons (barbed spears), spear throwers, and needles.

Needles were particularly important to early human society. Needles enabled people to sew garments out of animal hides and furs. This clothing kept people warm, so they could live in cold climates. Cro-Magnon people certainly needed this technology. They lived during the last ice age, which ended about ten thousand years ago. During this era, Earth was much colder than it is in the twenty-first century. Much of Europe was covered by sheets of ice.

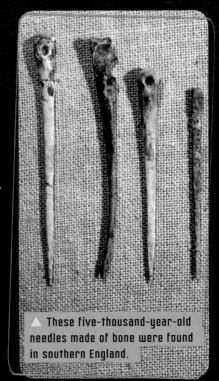

▲ These five-thousand-year-old needles made of bone were found in southern England.

Stonecutting tools are as old as human society. The first humans on Earth lived in eastern and southern Africa. They used stone blades to butcher meat and to cut grass, sticks, and bark. Archaeologists have found knapped stone tools in Ethiopia dating from 1.5 to 2 million years ago.

STONE ON STONE

Grinding tools were almost as important as cutting tools in ancient societies. Hunter-gatherers ground up seeds, nuts, plants, and grains to prepare flour, porridge, and other foods. The technique was simple. People crushed the plant materials between stones. They sometimes crushed chunks of soil, rock, and clay to make pigments, or paints.

Archaeologists have found fragments of ancient grinding stones in a trench in Cuddie Springs, Australia. These stones might be thirty thousand years old. Other early grinding stones come from Egypt and date to twenty thousand years ago. Both the Australian and the Egyptian grinding stones were made from sandstone, a soft rock.

▲ This mortar and pestle shaped from two stones was used for grinding wild grains into flour for cooking. It dates to around 9500 B.C. and is on display at a museum of antiquities outside of Paris, France.

Ancient peoples learned to shape grinding stones to fit neatly in their hands. These narrow rounded stones are called pestles. Ancient peoples also created mortars. These are curved stone slabs or cup-shaped vessels that hold material to grind up. A person worked the pestle against the seed, the grain, or other material inside the mortar to grind it up. The mortar provided a hard surface for grinding and also collected the crushed material.

BOWS FOR DRILLING

A bow is a two-part machine, consisting of a curved strip of material, with a cord called a bowstring connecting one end of the strip to the other. Early peoples made bows from wood. The cord that connected the two ends was made from a vine, a string of animal hide, or an animal tendon. Archaeologists think that people first used bows more than thirty thousand years ago in northern Africa.

When we think of bows, we usually think of bows and arrows, used as weapons. But the first bows were probably not weapons. They were drills. Here's how a bow drill worked: the bowstring was looped around a pointed shaft, such as a long, narrow stick or a stone. By moving the bow in a sawing (back-and-forth) motion, the operator could set the shaft spinning. The operator used the point of the spinning shaft to drill holes in wood, bone, or stone to make tools or ornaments.

This wall painting is from the tomb of Rekhmire, a high Egyptian official serving the pharaoh in the 1400s B.C. Carpenters use a bow drill to make holes in a table or a bench.

BOWS FOR STARTING FIRES

A bow drill's spinning movement creates friction at the tip of the drill. Friction occurs when objects rub together. Friction slows down moving objects. You can experience friction yourself by pressing the palms of your hands together and rubbing rapidly. Notice how the rubbing motion slows your hands a little. Do you also notice a warm feeling when you rub? Friction creates heat.

Ancient peoples understood that friction creates heat. They used this principle to start fires with bow drills. A person spun the shaft of a bow drill into a piece of wood. Soon the piece of wood got hot. It began to smolder, or burn without a flame. The person then placed dry leaves or wood chips on the smoldering wood. The leaves or wood chips soon started to burn.

BOWS AND ARROWS

Most modern people are familiar with the bow and arrow. An archer holds a bow in one hand. He or she draws back the bowstring and an arrow with the other hand. The archer's pull increases the bend of the bow. When the archer lets go of the bowstring, the bow springs back to its original shape. This quick unbending of the bow propels the arrow forward.

Ancient peoples began using bows and arrows at least twelve thousand years ago and probably much earlier. The best bows were made from the wood of yew trees. Yew offered just the right combination of strength and stretchiness needed in a bow. Arrows were made from shafts of wood. Arrowheads were made of sharpened stone or animal bone.

> "A bow kept taut will quickly break, but kept loosely strung, it will serve you when you need it."
>
> —Phaedrus, Roman writer, first century A.D.

Hunters on horseback pursue their prey with bows and arrows in this stone relief scene from the palace of Ashurbanipal. Ashurbanipal was king of the Assyrians from 668 to 627 B.C. He ruled from the ancient Assyrian city of Nineveh in modern-day Iraq.

People used bows and arrows to kill animals and sometimes to kill one another. Sudan, a modern country in north central Africa, has a burial ground called the Jebel Sahaba. The site dates from about 8000 B.C. Archaeologists found fifty-eight skeletons at the site. The dead included many women and children. The archaeologists also found many arrowheads embedded and mixed in among the bones. Archaeologists aren't sure what exactly happened at Jebel Sahaba, but it was probably the site of an ancient massacre in which the killers used bows and arrows.

CHAPTER TWO

THE ANCIENT MIDDLE EAST

Around 10,000 B.C., some people in the Middle East began to abandon the hunter-gatherer lifestyle. They settled down and became farmers. People built villages as well as big cities. Many people settled between the Tigris and Euphrates rivers, in a region later named Mesopotamia (which means "between rivers" in Greek). The area included most of modern Iraq and parts of modern Syria and Turkey.

Mesopotamia was home to a series of ancient civilizations, including the Sumerians, Babylonians, Hittites, and Assyrians. These and other ancient Middle Eastern peoples created many useful machines.

LEVERING WATER

Mesopotamians put the lever to good use on farms and in cities. To move water, they created a machine called a shadoof. This device was basically a lever. It consisted of a long pole balanced on top of an upright post. One end of the pole held a weight. The other end held a bucket. The upright post was the fulcrum. The shadoof operator dipped the bucket into a river or a ditch to scoop up water. The weight on the other end of the pole balanced the weight of the bucket of water. As the pole balanced in the air, the operator swung the bucket around to a new position. He or she then poured the water into an irrigation channel (a ditch for watering farmland) or a water storage tank or onto a garden. The first written description of a shadoof dates to about 2300 B.C. It comes from ancient Mesopotamia. Several ancient Egyptian wall paintings also show people using shadoofs.

An ancient Egyptian uses a shadoof to water plants. This modern painting is based on an original image from the tomb of a sculptor named Ipi in the ancient city of Thebes. The original picture dates to the 1200s B.C.

SIMPLE MACHINE: THE PULLEY

Have you ever pulled down on a rope to raise a flag to the top of a flagpole? If you have, then you've used a pulley. A pulley is one of the six simple machines. People in the ancient Middle East invented pulleys.

A pulley is a wheel with a grooved rim. The groove is designed to hold a rope or a chain. Imagine a tall pole with a pulley on top. A person threads a rope over the groove in the pulley and attaches a load to one end of the rope. By pulling on the other end of the rope, the person can lift the load. Pulleys make lifting loads easier. That's because a person pulling down uses his or her body weight to give extra force to the pull. Ancient peoples probably first used pulleys to hoist buckets of water from wells.

SIMPLE MACHINE: THE WHEEL AND AXLE

Mention wheels, and most people think of round devices on cars, bicycles, and other vehicles. Wheels turn around a center shaft called an axle.

It's true that wheels and axles are most commonly found on vehicles. But did you know that doorknobs, wrenches, screwdrivers, steering wheels, and water faucets are made of wheels and axles too?

A wheel and an axle are actually both wheels. One is bigger than the other. The axle is usually smaller than the wheel, but not always. Engineers think of the wheel and axle as one simple machine. Like other simple machines, the wheel and axle increases force.

To work this machine, a person applies force to the wheel. Turning the wheel also turns the axle. Did you ever try to turn a water faucet that was missing its handle? It is almost impossible to turn the slender stem (the axle). But the faucet's larger handle (the wheel) turns easily. That's because large wheels increase force more than small wheels. The easy-to-turn handle is attached to the hard-to-turn stem. The handle moves the stem with much less force than is needed to turn just the stem.

PUTTING THE WHEEL AND AXLE TO WORK

The Mesopotamians created the first wheeled vehicles around 3500 B.C. These were two- or four-wheeled wooden carts. People hitched the carts to oxen or other strong animals, which provided the necessary pulling power. The first pictures of wheeled carts are line drawings from the Sumerian city of Ur (in the southeast of modern-day Iraq). The drawings date from 3200 to 3100 B.C. Archaeologists have also found the remains of actual wooden wagons from Ur. The wagons date from 2600 to 2400 B.C.

Wheeled transportation revolutionized business, travel, warfare, and other aspects of ancient life. With wheeled vehicles, traders, armies, and other travelers could move more quickly and more efficiently. From Mesopotamia the wheel quickly spread to Europe and Asia.

▲ Horses pull a wheeled chariot in this stone carving from the Royal Tombs of Ur in modern-day Iraq. Archaeologists believe this carving to be one of the earliest known representations of the wheel.

The ancient Assyrians used the wheel and axle in a device called a windlass, or winch. It had a cranklike handle (the wheel) connected to a center axle and a length of rope. The rope could be attached to a heavy object. When a person turned the handle, the rope wrapped around the axle and hoisted the object. The Assyrians probably used windlasses to lift water from wells and dirt and metal from mines.

SPINNING

About eleven thousand years ago, ancient peoples began to domesticate animals. Domesticating is similar to taming. Domesticated animals live among humans instead of with their own wild relatives. After people domesticated sheep, they could shave off sheep's wool and turn it into cloth. But turning wool into cloth requires technology. That technology is spinning.

Most natural fibers are very short. Cotton fibers, for instance, are only about 0.5 inches (1.25 centimeters) long. Spinning changes short pieces of

fiber into long strands of thread or yarn. People weave or knit the strands together to make fabric.

Mesopotamians used machines called the spindle and the distaff to turn sheep's wool into yarn. The distaff is a small stick with a slot on one end. The slot holds clumps of wool. The spindle is a long straight stick held between thumb and index finger. By twirling the spindle, a person can carefully draw fibers off the distaff. The short wool fibers cling and twist together. They become a long strand of yarn.

To maintain the momentum, or continuous motion, of the spindle, ancient peoples attached it to a small clay disk called a whorl. The whorl stored up energy as it spun. It kept the spindle rotating at a constant speed.

THE POTTER'S WHEEL

Pottery making is an old technology. The first evidence of pottery making comes from ancient Japan. People there made pottery as early as 14,000 B.C. For centuries the primary tool for pottery making was the human hand. People pinched balls of clay into bowls or jars. Or they rolled out long ropes of clay and coiled them to create the walls of a pot. Potters fired the vessels in hot ovens to harden the clay.

Around 3500 B.C., about the same time people invented wheels for transportation, people in Mesopotamia invented the potter's wheel. The first potter's wheel was probably just a simple wooden turntable. The potter turned the wheel slowly while creating the walls of a coiled pot. The turning wheel allowed the potter to stack the coils more evenly and faster than could be done by hand alone.

Ancient peoples soon built heavier and faster turntables, made from stone. They probably greased the axles to minimize friction. With less friction, a wheel would keep turning for a long time after one good push. A potter could then wet a lump of clay, spin the wheel, make an indentation in the center of the spinning clay, and squeeze inside and out to form the walls of a pot. This new technique was called throwing.

One of the earliest images of ancient pottery making comes from an Egyptian tomb. The wall painting shows potters softening clay with their hands and feet, shaping it on turntables, and firing it in kilns, or ovens. The painting dates to 1970 B.C.

▶ An Egyptian model from around 2500 B.C. shows a potter throwing pots on a wheel.

METALS MAKE BETTER MACHINES

Ancient peoples made many machines from stone, bone, and wood. They also used metals to craft more powerful and more efficient machines. Metals are stronger and last longer than stone, bone, and wood. They also have a property called plasticity. Plasticity is the ability to be melted, bent, stretched, shaped, and reshaped without breaking. Plasticity is very important to machine makers.

People in Mesopotamia used copper as early as 8000 B.C. But getting copper from the ground is not easy. Ancient peoples couldn't just dig up big lumps of copper from a mine. Copper is almost always combined with other substances inside rocks. To get the copper, ancient craftspeople had to remove it from the rock.

A rock that contains a valuable metal is called an ore. Separating metal from its ore involves smelting. The process requires high-temperature furnaces. The high heat burns off some of the ore and melts the metal, which falls to the bottom of the furnace. Science historians think that peoples in ancient Anatolia (modern-day Turkey) and Mesopotamia were the first ones to smelt copper ore.

▲ Two copper nails, one with a ringed head, date to 2600 B.C. They were found in the ancient Sumarian city of Mari, near the Euphrates River.

Copper is a soft metal. Once ancient peoples separated it from its ore, they hammered it to shape it. They sometimes heated copper in furnaces to make it even softer and easier to shape. They created copper tools, weapons, and ornaments.

STRONGER METALS

Bronze is an alloy, or mixture, of copper, tin, and sometimes other metals. It is made by melting the different metals in a furnace, mixing them together when still hot, and allowing the mixture to cool. In the 3000s B.C., craftspeople in Mesopotamia and Anatolia learned to make bronze. They found that bronze was harder, stronger, and more durable than pure copper.

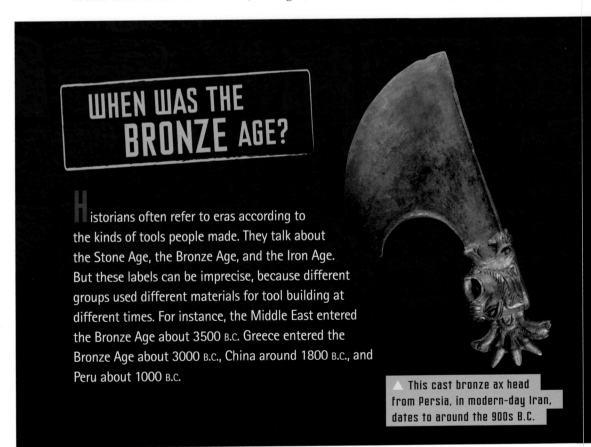

WHEN WAS THE
BRONZE AGE?

Historians often refer to eras according to the kinds of tools people made. They talk about the Stone Age, the Bronze Age, and the Iron Age. But these labels can be imprecise, because different groups used different materials for tool building at different times. For instance, the Middle East entered the Bronze Age about 3500 B.C. Greece entered the Bronze Age about 3000 B.C., China around 1800 B.C., and Peru about 1000 B.C.

▲ This cast bronze ax head from Persia, in modern-day Iran, dates to around the 900s B.C.

This is one of thirteen bronze panels that were nailed to the gates of the Assyrian Temple of Mamu in modern-day Iraq. The scenes commemorate important events of the day in the 800s B.C. These cast bronze panels, are on display at the British Museum in London.

They also found that bronze could be easily cast. Casting involves melting metal into liquid form, pouring it into a mold, and letting it harden. If a craftsperson in ancient times broke a bronze tool, he could easily melt it and recast it into another tool. Peoples in the ancient Middle East made bronze tools, weapons, and armor.

Iron is stronger and harder than bronze. It is rarely found in pure form. Usually people must smelt iron ore to get iron. In about 1200 B.C., the Hittites began to smelt iron ore. They created iron spears and battle-axes. These weapons gave them an advantage over enemies who used softer bronze weapons.

> "Iron is taken from the earth, and copper
> is smelted from ore."

—Hebrew Bible

Making iron tools was hard for people in the ancient Middle East. If they wanted to cast iron, they had to melt it first. Iron melts at about 2,800°F (1,538°C). But the furnaces in the ancient Middle East could not reach that temperature. So Middle Eastern craftspeople found another way to work with iron. They heated it in furnaces to soften it. When the iron was red hot, a craftsperson pulled it from the furnace and pounded it into shape with heavy hammers. Iron shaped by pounding is called wrought iron.

THE **INDIANS** DID IT **FIRST**

People in ancient India created the first spinning wheel. Instead of a small whorl, this machine had a large wheel to turn the spindle. The invention dates to 500 B.C.

The ancient Indians were also the first people to use steel. Steel is iron with extra carbon in it. The extra carbon makes steel stronger and more durable than ordinary iron.

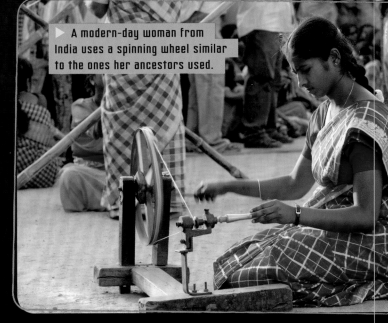

▶ A modern-day woman from India uses a spinning wheel similar to the ones her ancestors used.

THE FIRST MACHINE TOOL

Machine tools are the basis of modern industry. Modern machine tools are usually large, power-driven devices. Craftspeople use them to cut and shape metal, wood, and plastic. People often use machine tools to make other tools. Archaeologists think the first machine tool came from the ancient Middle East. This tool was the lathe.

Lathes have sharp blades. A craftsperson who wants to cut something with a lathe first places the object on a spindle. As the spindle rotates, the object rubs against the sharp blade of the lathe. The blade peels and scrapes away

King Darius (550–486 B.C.) of Persia receives visitors. The legs of his chair have been turned on a lathe. This limestone relief carving adorns the walls of the royal treasury building in Persepolis, the ancient Persian capital located in modern-day Iran.

A relief carving from 1000 B.C. depicts a Babylonian carpenter at work. Carpenters used many tools, including lathes, to shape wood into useful and decorative objects.

excess wood or metal, giving the object the desired shape. Craftspeople often use lathes to carve decorative, rounded wooden legs for chairs and other furniture.

Archaeologists aren't sure when the lathe was invented. Some evidence comes from ancient Turkey. There, archaeologists have found wooden plates dating to the 800s B.C. They appear to have been shaped by a lathe. Carvings and paintings from other parts of the ancient Middle East show furniture that was probably cut with lathes.

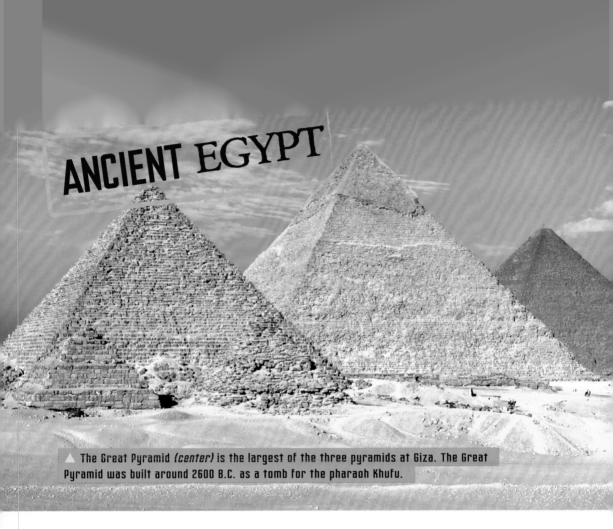

ANCIENT EGYPT

The Great Pyramid *(center)* is the largest of the three pyramids at Giza. The Great Pyramid was built around 2600 B.C. as a tomb for the pharaoh Khufu.

Ancient Egypt is famous for its giant pyramids. The pyramids are tombs of Egyptian pharaohs, or rulers. The largest pyramid, the Great Pyramid, is the tomb of Pharaoh Khufu. It was built at the city of Giza around 2600 B.C. The Great Pyramid is 481 feet (147 meters) high. Each side of its base is 756 feet (230 m) long. That's longer than two and a half football fields. Builders used two million blocks of limestone to make the pyramid. Most blocks weighed about 3.5 tons (3.2 metric tons) each.

When they built the pyramids, the Egyptians knew about only three simple machines. These machines were the lever, the wedge, and the inclined plane. They didn't know about the pulley, the wheel and axle, or the screw. How did the Egyptians build pyramids with only three simple machines? How did workers raise heavy stone blocks into position as a pyramid rose hundreds of feet above the ground?

SIMPLE MACHINE: THE INCLINED PLANE

An inclined plane is a flat surface that slopes up and down. It sounds so simple that it might be hard to believe an inclined plane is really a machine. But the inclined plane is actually one of the most important machines for moving heavy loads to a higher level. Have you ever seen someone wheel a washing machine or refrigerator up a metal ramp into a truck? That ramp is an inclined plane.

Archaeologists have found the remains of earthen ramps at several pyramid sites. They think builders used these inclined planes to drag blocks to high levels in pyramids. As a pyramid rose higher, workers built the ramps higher. They tore the ramps down when the pyramid was finished.

▼ A ramp to the pyramid of Abu Rawash is visible in this aerial photograph taken about 5 miles (8 kilometers) north of Giza. Khufu's son Djedefre was buried here in 2558 B.C. Many of the limestone blocks that made up the pyramid have been stolen over time.

DON'T BELIEVE EVERYTHING YOU READ

The Greek historian Herodotus (ca. 484–425 B.C.) wrote about life in ancient Egypt. He explained how workers built the Great Pyramid:

> The pyramid was built in steps. . . . After laying the stones for the base, they raised the remaining stones to their places by means of machines formed of short wooden planks [levers]. The first machine raised them from the ground to the top of the first step. On this there was another machine, which received the stone upon its arrival, and conveyed it to the second step, whence [from where] a third machine advanced it still higher.

For centuries, people relied on Herodotus's description of pyramid building. Archaeologists searched for evidence that workers used levers to lift the giant stone blocks from one level of a pyramid to the next. But archaeologists never found any evidence in Egyptian art or writing to show that the giant stone blocks were raised according to Herodotus's description.

Herodotus also wrote that one hundred thousand men built the Great Pyramid over twenty years. But modern archaeologists think the tomb was built much more quickly, with much less labor. The remains of the workers' barracks at the pyramid site show that it would have housed a staff of only four thousand.

Herodotus wrote about events in Egypt about two thousand years after they happened. Any historian writing about events thousands of years before his or her time is bound to make some mistakes. In addition, Herodotus got his information as a tourist would. He visited Egypt and talked to the local people. His information was only as accurate as the stories he heard.

▼ A carving from 700 B.C. shows workers building a palace for Assyrian king Sennacherib. At the bottom of the picture, slaves use a giant lever to move a stone block onto a sledge. Similar techniques were used by the ancient Egyptians to move enormous stone blocks from quarries to building sites.

MECHANICAL ADVANTAGE

How helpful is a machine to a person lifting a load? Engineers answer that question by talking about mechanical advantage. Mechanical advantage is the amount of help a machine provides in doing work. For example, if a lever allows you to move a 200-pound (90-kilogram) stone with just 50 pounds (23 kg) of force, then the lever has multiplied your force by four. The mechanical advantage of that lever is four.

In the case of the inclined plane, mechanical advantage is equal to the length of the plane divided by the height the object must be raised. So if you needed to raise a refrigerator 6 feet (1.8 m) into a truck, a 6-foot ramp would be of no help. Its mechanical advantage (6 divided by 6) would be only 1. With an 18-foot (5.5 m) ramp, however, loading the refrigerator would be a breeze. The ramp's mechanical advantage (18 divided by 6) would be 3: for every 3 pounds (1.4 kg) of load, the mover would need to exert only 1 pound (0. 5 kg) of force.

The example shows that the longer the inclined plane, the more the mechanical advantage. The ancient Egyptians used ramps that were hundreds—even thousands—of feet long. This was the only way to gain the mechanical advantage needed to move giant stones to great heights.

MORE BUILDING MACHINES

Egyptian builders used a variety of other machines besides inclined planes. Before they could build pyramids, laborers had to cut large limestone slabs from stone quarries. Stonecutters devised a clever way of splitting the slabs. First, they inserted wooden wedges into natural cracks in the rock. Or they drilled a line of holes into the rock and drove wedges into the holes. Then workers soaked the wedges with water. Wood swells when wet. So the wedges swelled up and enlarged the cracks and holes in the rock. After about ten hours, the stonecutters inserted larger wooden wedges. They repeated the process until a slab of rock broke free.

To move the big stone blocks to building sites, workers floated them on river barges. At construction sites, people probably dragged the stones on sledges. Sledges are rectangular platforms that slide across the ground.

▲ This Egyptian painting from around 1000 B.C. shows workers dragging limestone blocks on a sledge.

▲ Ancient Egyptian stoneworkers carry blocks, stone carving tools, and buckets. This carving from around 2400 B.C. was found in a tomb at Saqqara.

Ancient Egyptians probably put narrow runners on the undersides of sledges to reduce friction. With less material touching the ground, less friction built up. The sledge could move faster.

As pyramids grew higher during construction, workers used sledges to haul stones up earthen ramps. They probably used bronze and wooden levers to maneuver the big blocks into their correct positions in the high pyramid wall. For the more detailed work of shaping and carving stones, Egyptian craftspeople used copper and bronze chisels and saws.

"I have made me [a] house, adorned with gold, its ceilings with lapis lazuli [a blue stone], its walls having deep foundations. Its doors are of copper, their bolts are of bronze. It is made for everlasting; eternity is in awe of it."

—Amenemhet I, Egyptian pharaoh, 1900s B.C.

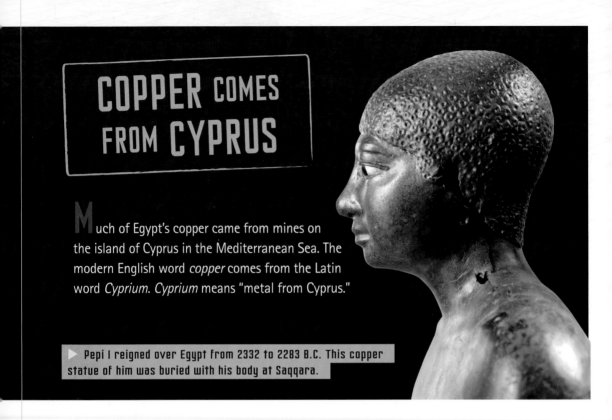

COPPER COMES FROM CYPRUS

Much of Egypt's copper came from mines on the island of Cyprus in the Mediterranean Sea. The modern English word *copper* comes from the Latin word *Cyprium*. *Cyprium* means "metal from Cyprus."

▶ Pepi I reigned over Egypt from 2332 to 2283 B.C. This copper statue of him was buried with his body at Saqqara.

Who figured out how to cut giant stone slabs with wedges and move them using sledges, levers, and inclined planes? No one knows for sure. But Imhotep, adviser to the pharaoh Djoser, might have played a role. Around 2650 B.C., Imhotep supervised construction of the Step Pyramid at Saqqara. This was the first pyramid built in Egypt. Manetho, an Egyptian priest and historian, called Imhotep the "inventor of the art of building in hewn [cut] stone."

BEYOND THE PYRAMIDS

Because of the pyramids, ancient Egypt will always be associated with large-scale building projects. People will always marvel at how Egyptians built massive buildings with just three simple machines. But Egyptian craftspeople also worked on a smaller scale. They created many machines to help them with day-to-day work.

Looms are frames for weaving cloth. To get started, weavers string a set of threads lengthwise on a loom. These threads are called the warp. Weavers then interlace another set of threads across the warp. These threads are the weft. Archaeologists think that people in eastern Europe created the first looms around 6000 B.C. People in different cultures improved on the basic loom design. The ancient Egyptians, for example, added the heddle. This movable device keeps threads of the warp separated from one another, making it easier to weave the weft between them.

▼ This modern painting is based on a scene originally created in the 1700s or 1600s B.C. The picture shows ancient Egyptians weaving *(left)* and spinning *(right)*.

While people in almost every ancient culture used paddles to power boats, the ancient Egyptians were probably the first ones to use rudders. Rudders are flat boards used to steer boats. They are usually made of wood. Like oars and paddles, they are levers. One end of the lever holds a handle, called a tiller. The other end of the lever sits in the water. The back edge of the boat acts as the fulcrum. When a sailor moves the tiller to the right or left, the other end of the rudder moves in the opposite direction. It presses against the water. This action turns the boat in one direction or the other. Archaeologists have found the remains of ancient Egyptian boats, rudders, and models of boats. These artifacts (remains of a human culture) show that rudders were common in ancient Egypt.

▼ This model boat, complete with a rudder, was buried in a tomb around 1900 B.C. Boats inside tombs were supposed to transport dead people to the afterlife.

Another useful machine from ancient Egypt was the water clock, or clepsydra. Before this invention, ancient people used sundials to tell time. A sundial is a flat disk with a style, or stick, in the center. When sunlight hits a sundial, the shadow of the style falls on a certain spot on the dial. As the sun moves across the sky, the shadow moves across the dial. Ancient peoples told time by marking the position of the shadow on a sundial. But the device had many flaws. For one thing, it didn't work at night or on cloudy days. The clepsydra worked day or night. This simple device was made from a pottery jar. It had horizontal markings on the inside and a small hole at the bottom. At sunset a person filled the jar with water. The water flowed through the hole in the bottom of the jar at a constant rate. As the water dripped out, one marking after another became visible inside the jar. Each marking that appeared meant that another period of time had passed. Ancient Egyptians built the first clepsydra around 1500 B.C. Water clocks spread from Egypt and became common in other ancient cultures.

CHAPTER FOUR

ANCIENT CHINA

China is one of the world's oldest ancient cultures. It dates to about 10,000 B.C. The ancient Chinese developed some well-known technology. This technology includes papermaking, silk making, and acupuncture (inserting fine needles into the skin to treat pain or sickness). The ancient Chinese also built the Great Wall of China to protect themselves from northern invaders. This landmark of construction technology runs almost all the way across northern China.

Chinese contributions to machine building are not as well known. For centuries China was isolated from the rest of the ancient world. The Chinese

▼ The ancient Chinese built the Great Wall to keep out enemy invadors. Portions of the wall were built as early as the 5th century B.C. The majority of the wall that still stands was built during the Ming Dynasty (1368–1644).

did not know about technology developed in the Middle East, Egypt, Europe, or the Americas. So the Chinese came up with their own mechanical solutions to common problems. Independently, they developed much of the same machinery as other ancient groups.

THE WOODEN OX

The ancient Chinese developed one machine long before the rest of the world. They called it the "wooden ox" or the "gliding horse." We call this machine the wheelbarrow.

The wheelbarrow combines two simple machines: the lever and the wheel and axle. The platform and handles of the wheelbarrow make up the lever. When a person applies force, by lifting the handles, the platform lifts the load. The wheel and axle act as the fulcrum. They pivot beneath the load. They also allow the wheelbarrow to roll easily.

The wheelbarrow's origins are unclear. Legends say that a Chinese general invented the wheelbarrow around A.D. 230. But archaeologists think that Chinese people actually invented wheelbarrows several centuries earlier.

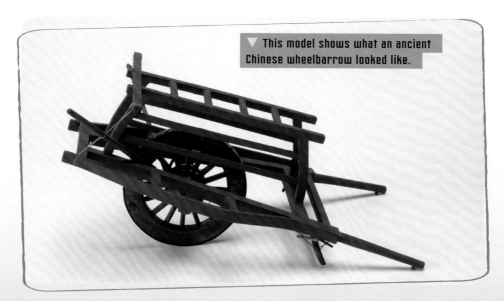

▼ This model shows what an ancient Chinese wheelbarrow looked like.

> **"Zhu-ge Liang invented machines, namely the wooden ox and gliding horse, that were powered neither by the wind nor water, and the wooden ox and gliding horse carried loads without need of man's physical effort."**
>
> — *Book of Qi*, A.D. 500s

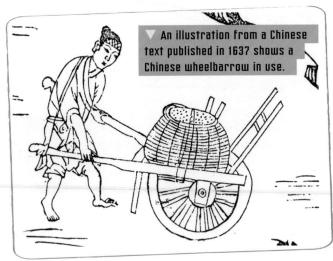

▼ An illustration from a Chinese text published in 1637 shows a Chinese wheelbarrow in use.

No matter who invented it, the wheelbarrow was an inexpensive, simple, easy-to-maintain machine for transporting food and equipment. With a wheelbarrow, one soldier could transport enough food to supply four soldiers for three months. The Chinese used wheelbarrows to move rice, vegetables, and even people. Some Chinese wheelbarrows could hold several passengers.

CASTING IRON

Craftspeople in the ancient Middle East could not get iron hot enough to melt it. So they could not cast iron. Instead, they used wrought iron, which is weaker and less sturdy than cast iron. The ancient Chinese were able to melt and cast iron. They developed the process around 400 B.C. Other groups didn't learn to cast iron until hundreds of years later.

Why were the Chinese able to melt iron when other groups could not? Geological factors helped in the process. In China iron ore contains large

▲ This mold was used for casting iron sickle blades. Sickles are farming tools used for harvesting. Found by archaeologists in China in 1953, the iron mold dates to around 400 B.C.

amounts of phosphorus. This kind of ore melts at a lower temperature than iron ore in the Middle East. Sometimes the Chinese added extra phosphorus to iron ore during heating. China also has clay that can withstand very high temperatures. Chinese craftspeople used this clay to build furnaces for melting iron.

The Chinese used cast iron to make sturdy weapons, farm tools, and cooking pots. They even made a pagoda, or temple, out of cast iron.

THE BELLOWS HELPS OUT

The ancient Chinese created a machine to assist them in casting iron. That machine was the bellows. A bellows makes wind. It has a chamber that sucks in air and a valve for letting the air out. When a person presses on the air-filled chamber, air rushes out through the valve.

Have you ever blown on glowing coals in a barbecue? The oxygen from your breath makes the coals burn hotter. You can also use a bellows to make a fire burn hotter. The ancient Chinese did just that.

In the 200s B.C., the Chinese developed hand-operated bellows that produced strong currents of air. Metalworkers used these bellows to make their iron furnaces burn hotter.

Around A.D. 30, a Chinese government official named Tu Shih invented a water-powered bellows. This complicated machine contained gears, axles, and levers. It was much more powerful than hand-operated bellows. The power for the machine came from a waterwheel. A waterwheel gets its power from moving water, such as water flowing in a river.

ANCIENT CYBERNETICS

Have you ever heard of a science called cybernetics? It deals with automatic control systems in machines, living things, and even businesses. The autopilot system on an airplane is an example of cybernetics. The system uses feedback from the environment to control the machine. For instance, an autopilot might detect that an airplane is flying too low to the ground. The autopilot then steers the plane to the correct altitude. The word *cybernetics* comes from the Greek word *kybernetes*. It means "pilot," or "governor."

The ancient Chinese developed the first cybernetic machine. It was called the south-pointing carriage. Experts aren't sure who invented the carriage or when. Some people date its invention to 1030 B.C. Others think it was invented in the third century A.D.

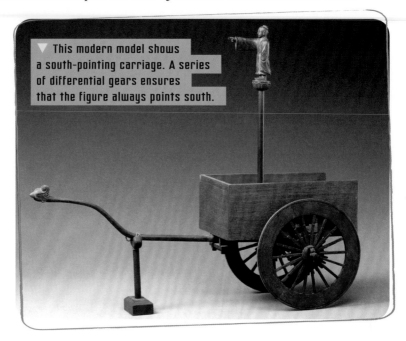

▼ This modern model shows a south-pointing carriage. A series of differential gears ensures that the figure always points south.

In many ways, the south-pointing carriage was an ordinary wagon. It was designed to be pulled by animals. It had ordinary wooden wheels. But the carriage had an unusual jade statue mounted on top. The statue was the figure of a Chinese sage, or wise man. He stood with one arm extended, pointing in front of him.

Between its wheels, the carriage was unusual in another way. Its wheels were connected by a series of gears to the jade statue. No matter which way the carriage turned, the statue always turned in response, so that its arm always pointed south. The statue helped travelers find their way. One Chinese historian described the vehicle:

> The south-pointing carriage was first constructed by the Duke of Zhou as a means of conducting homewards certain envoys [foreign representatives] who had arrived from a great distance beyond the frontiers. The country was a boundless plain in which people lost their bearings as to east and west, so the Duke caused this vehicle to be made in order that the ambassadors should be able to distinguish north and south.

Did the south-pointing carriage contain a magnetic compass (a device for determining direction)? No. The south-pointing carriage contained a series of complex gears called differential gears.

Cars have differential gears. For a car to turn a corner, the outer and inner wheels must turn at different speeds and travel different distances. The outer wheels have to travel farther than the inner wheels. A car's differential system senses the need for these different speeds and distances.

Gears in the south-pointing carriage worked much like modern differential gears. They sensed changes in the carriage's direction. They provided feedback to other gears and always kept the statue pointing south.

AN ANCIENT SEISMOGRAPH

Modern scientists measure earthquakes with machines called seismographs. These instruments are extremely sensitive. They can detect movements under the ground as small as 0.1 nanometer. A nanometer is one hundred thousand times smaller than the width of a human hair.

Chang Heng, a Chinese scientist, built a seismograph in A.D. 132. His machine could not measure tiny ground movements. But it could tell people when and where an earthquake had occurred. Chang Heng called his device an earthquake weathercock (*above*).

The earthquake weathercock was a big jar measuring 6 feet (1.8 m) across. The top of the jar had eight carved dragon heads. Each dragon faced one of the main directions of the compass: north, south, east, west, northeast, southeast, northwest, or southwest. Each dragon also held a ball in its mouth. Below the dragons, at the base of the jar, were eight carved toads. Each toad had an open mouth. When an earthquake occurred, one of the eight dragons released its ball into the mouth of the toad below. People noted which toad caught the ball to learn where the earthquake had taken place.

Ancient writers didn't explain what happened inside the jar to trigger the balls to fall. Modern scientists think the jar contained an upside-down pendulum. This was a thin spike attached to the bottom of the jar but swinging freely at the top. When the pendulum moved with Earth, the pendulum pushed a ball out of one of the dragon's throats. A Chinese historian tells this story about the earthquake weathercock:

On one occasion one of the dragons let fall a ball from its mouth though no perceptible shock [earthquake] could be felt. . . . But several days later a messenger arrived bringing news of an earthquake in Lung-Hsi [400 miles or 644 km away]. Upon this, everyone admitted the mysterious power of the instrument.

A BETTER BOW

Like most early peoples, the ancient Chinese used bows and arrows for both hunting and warfare. In the 300s B.C., the Chinese improved on the ordinary bow. They created the crossbow. A crossbow is similar to an ordinary bow. But it has a crank or a lever for drawing back the bowstring and arrow. An archer doesn't have to pull on the string using muscle power alone. The crossbow offers advantages over ordinary bows. For one thing, crossbows can be bigger and stronger than ordinary bows, since machines help people operate them. Crossbows can shoot arrows farther and with more force than ordinary bows.

In addition, crossbows have a catch to hold the bowstring in a cocked position. So an archer can hold the bow, ready to shoot, as long as needed, with less strain on the muscles. With the catch doing the work of holding the bowstring, the archer doesn't have to rush to take a shot and is more likely to hit the target.

Chinese historians first wrote about archers using crossbows at the Battle of Ma-Ling in 341 B.C. At this fight between two warring Chinese states, an army of ten thousand crossbowmen nearly wiped out the opposing force. The oldest actual crossbow ever found comes from the tomb of Wu-Yang, a Chinese prince. It dates to 228 B.C.

▶ An illustration from 1300s China shows two Chinese warriors training with crossbows. Chinese soldiers used crossbows in battle for hundreds of years.

THE ANCIENT AMERICAS

Ancient American cultures developed independently from those in Europe, the Middle East, Africa, and Asia. Ancient societies in North, South, and Central America had little if any contact with people from other continents. So they had no way to learn about technologies in distant lands. After people in Mesopotamia invented the wheel, the technology spread east to China and west to Europe. But people in the ancient Americas didn't learn about the new invention.

When Ancient Americans wanted to solve problems, they had to come up with technology on their own. They learned by trial and error. Although

▼ The Inca built magnificent cities, such as Machu Picchu in Peru, with only three of six simple machines.

ancient Americans built impressive buildings and vast road networks, they created far fewer machines than people in other parts of the world.

SET IN STONE?

Ancient American cultures mainly used tools made of stone or wood instead of metal. It's not that ancient Americans didn't use metal at all. They just never used metal to make big machines. Ancient peoples in North America hammered copper to make small decorations. By 2000 B.C., people in the Andes Mountains of South America knew how to smelt copper from ore. People in both Central and South America fashioned ornaments from copper, silver, and gold.

Ancient Inuit people, who lived in the far north of North America, made knives and spearheads from pure iron. Iron in its pure form (not mixed in ore) is rare on Earth. Some of the iron came from meteorites. These rocky objects had crashed into Earth from outer space. Other iron came from natural iron deposits on a small island near Greenland.

In Peru in South America, people learned to make bronze in about 1000 B.C. They made the metal by combining local copper with tin from the Andes Mountains. Technically, Peru entered the

▶ Ancient Americans used metal to create ornamental pieces and small tools, but not large machines. This gold ornament dates to the Inca Empire (1200–1500).

Bronze Age at this point. But many archaeologists don't consider it a real Bronze Age, because the ancient Peruvians made only small bronze tools and ornaments. They never made large bronze tools or weapons.

RAZOR SHARP

Ancient Americans made effective machines even though they didn't use much metal. Their weapons were sharp and deadly. For instance, the ancient Aztec people, based in modern-day Mexico, made war clubs called *macuahuitls*. The clubs were mostly made of wood. The edges of the clubs were lined with small, sharp pieces of obsidian. This natural glass comes from the lava that flows from volcanoes.

▲ A sixteenth-century Spanish chronicler made this drawing of Aztec warriors dressed in eagle and jaguar costumes and wielding macuahuitls.

A HOLE IN THE HEAD

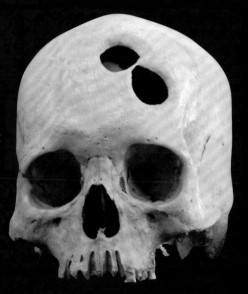

Ancient brain surgery might sound like a far-out idea. But the surgery was widespread in ancient societies, especially in ancient South America.

To perform brain surgery, ancient surgeons cut or drilled holes in patients' skulls. The process is called trepanning. Surgeons used different kinds of tools to perform the task. The bow drill was the most common.

Sometimes doctors performed brain surgery on people we would call mentally ill. But in ancient times, people didn't understand mental illness. Surgeons trepanned these patients to let

▲ Ancient surgeons used knives or bow drills to perform brain surgery.

"evil spirits" escape from their heads. Ancient surgeons also trepanned skulls to treat headaches, seizures, and other ailments. They often used the procedure to treat skull fractures. Trepanning allowed surgeons to clean out bits of shattered bone and pools of blood from fractured skulls. Ancient surgeons had to be careful to cut only through the skull, not into the brain. After the operation, the surgeon covered the hole in the skull with a shell or a piece of gourd.

Some ancient brain operations were certainly failures. Many patients likely died from infections after surgery. But other operations were successful. Archaeologists have studied hundreds of trepanned skulls from around the world. More than half of the skulls show signs of new bone growth after the operations. The growth is evidence that the patients survived the procedure and started to heal.

The greatest number of ancient trepanned skulls comes from Peru and Bolivia in South America. One ancient Peruvian knife contains three carved figurines on its handle. One of the figures appears to be cutting into another's head. The knife was probably used for trepanning.

The Aztecs and other ancient Americans crafted other tools out of stone, animal bone, animal horn, and plant fibers. They used simple looms to weave elaborate textiles. They spun yarn with spindles and whorls.

REINVENTING THE WHEEL

Like other early peoples, ancient Americans relied on simple machines to get work done. They used wedges such as knives and chisels. They made levers such as digging sticks and paddles. The ancient Inca, who ruled a vast empire in South America, also used the inclined plane. Like the ancient Egyptians, the Inca built earthen ramps for hauling stone blocks into place at construction projects.

Ancient Americans did not devise the screw or the pulley. And they used only small wheels such as spindle whorls. They did not make pottery on wheels. Nor did they build wheels for transportation. Experts have pointed out that wheeled carts would not have done ancient Americans much good anyway, because the Americas did not have big strong animals, such as oxen, to pull them.

Interestingly, the peoples of ancient Mesoamerica (Mexico and Central America) envisioned wheeled vehicles, even if they didn't use them. Archaeologists have found toy animals from ancient Mesoamerica with

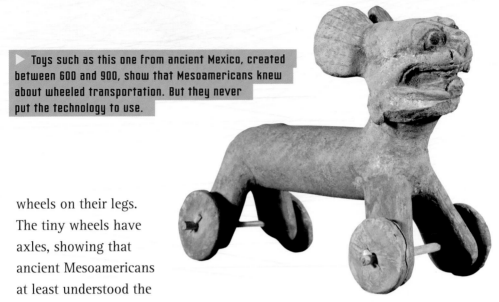

▶ Toys such as this one from ancient Mexico, created between 600 and 900, show that Mesoamericans knew about wheeled transportation. But they never put the technology to use.

wheels on their legs. The tiny wheels have axles, showing that ancient Mesoamericans at least understood the concept of wheeled transportation. The toys, made from clay, were mostly in the shape of dogs, monkeys, and wild cats. They date from A.D. 200s and later.

GET UP AND GO

If the ancient Americans didn't use wheels for transportation, how did they carry heavy loads and move stones to build temples and other structures? In many cases, they used human muscle power alone, with large groups of laborers dragging or carrying loads. Some archaeologists think the Inca might have used log rollers to move heavy stones. This process would have involved rolling a stone over a series of logs. As the stone moved along, people would have had to move logs from the back of the stone to the front to keep it rolling.

Throughout the Americas, ancient peoples also relied on pack animals to carry heavy loads. In South America, the most common pack animal was the llama, a member of the camel family. Some ancient North Americans dragged their possessions from place to place on travois. These were sledges made of two long poles with a net or wooden platform between them for carrying gear. People hitched travois to dogs (and later horses) to pull the load. Toboggans originated among the ancient peoples of North America. These were sledges that traveled over snow. Dogs and sometimes people on snowshoes provided the pulling power.

ANCIENT GREECE

This detail from a Greek vase from the 700s B.C. shows two blacksmiths using a furnace to heat metal for shaping.

The ancient Greeks believed that twelve powerful gods ruled the world from Mount Olympus, a snow-covered peak in northern Greece. In Greek paintings and sculptures, one of these gods usually looks dirty and rough. The dirty god is Hephaestus, god of fire and metalworking. He makes machines and other objects from metal.

Greece was one of the most learned societies of the ancient world. It was home to great philosophers, writers, and artists. Some Greeks thought that engineering was a lowly craft. They thought it was beneath the dignity of educated people. This attitude didn't seem to discourage Greek builders and engineers, however. They created some of the most impressive machines of ancient times.

SIMPLE MACHINE: THE SCREW

Ancient Greek culture arose in about 750 B.C. By this time, five of the six simple machines had been invented. The Greeks invented the sixth simple machine and used it in many technologies. That machine was the screw.

The screw is based on another simple machine, the inclined plane. The threads, or ridges, on a screw provide mechanical advantage, just as an inclined plane does. But instead of aiding movement in a straight line, screw threads allow movement in a spiral.

People often use screws as fastening devices. You've probably used screws to attach two pieces of wood or metal. Turning a screw provides the force that presses the two pieces of material together. People also use screws to lift loads. For instance, some jacks that lift cars and other heavy objects are actually large screws.

GRAPES AND OLIVES

Ancient Greek farmers grew lots of different crops. Two of the most common were grapes and olives. The Greeks crushed grapes to make wine and crushed olives to make olive oil.

▲ The ancient Greeks used screw presses and other technology to crush grapes into wine. Modern Greece is still a grape-growing region.

To crush these fruits, they used a machine called a press. Early presses were operated by winches. Winch-driven presses weren't very powerful.

The ancient Greeks created a better press called a screw press. This press combined two simple machines, the screw and the lever. The screw portion of the press was mounted upright. Turning it put upward pressure on the lever. As one end of the lever moved up, the opposite end moved down. The downward-moving section of the lever squeezed olives or grapes inside a container.

Greek screw presses were large machines. Some of the biggest ones were turned by oxen. Others were operated by a single person turning the screw. These presses squeezed much more juice and oil out of fruit than earlier, winch-driven presses.

In the first century A.D., a Greek inventor named Hero made the screw press even better. His press didn't have a lever. It used the screw to apply force directly to grapes and olives. Cutting out the lever cut down on friction. That change made Hero's screw press more forceful and more efficient than earlier screw presses. Hero's press squeezed out even more grape juice and olive oil.

A GREAT INVENTOR

Hero invented other remarkable machines. One machine pumped water in a steady stream, much like a modern fire hose. The pump used a complicated system of valves, chambers, and moving parts to keep the water flowing.

Another of Hero's inventions was the aeolipile. It was a simple steam engine. It had a chamber filled with water. When heated, the water turned into steam. The steam traveled through tubes into a hollow metal ball. Two more tubes extended from opposite sides of the ball. Their ends were bent at right angles. As steam hissed out of these tubes, the force of the steam spun the ball around.

Another invention was a small windmill. Hero used it to blow air into a toy organ. He also used weights, strings, and rotating drums to build a miniature theater. The theater even contained mechanical dolls, which put on a play.

Hero could have put his devices to practical use. For instance, his steam engine could have powered machinery. But Hero apparently didn't care about practical uses for his machines. He used his inventions as toys.

▶ This is a reconstruction of Hero's invention the aeolipile, the first steam engine.

ANCIENT R&D

Many twenty-first century advances in technology, business, and government come from research and development (R&D) programs. In these programs, experts work together to study problems and come up with solutions. The experts set goals, conduct experiments, and run tests. They use the results of their tests and studies to build new products.

An ancient Greek ruler named Dionysius the Elder might have organized the world's first R&D program. Dionysius ruled Syracuse from 405 to 367 B.C. This Greek-controlled city was on the island of Sicily in the Mediterranean Sea. In 399 B.C., Dionysius needed new weapons to prepare Syracuse for war with Carthage, a powerful city-state on the northern coast of Africa.

A famous story says that Dionysius assembled large teams of military specialists. He broke their assignment into small parts and assigned one part to each team. He gave his experts cash bonuses for accomplishing their goals on time. He frequently reminded them that the safety of their homeland, families, and friends depended on the results of their research.

According to the story, Dionysius's team invented the catapult. A catapult is a large war machine. It hurls rocks, spears, arrows, and other missiles at an enemy force. Catapults operate much like handheld bows and crossbows. But they are many times larger.

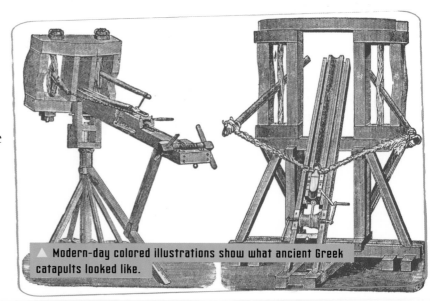
Modern-day colored illustrations show what ancient Greek catapults looked like.

CTESIBIUS of ALEXANDRIA

Alexandria, Egypt, was a center of art, learning, and science in the ancient world. Many Greek scholars made their homes in Alexandria because of its strong ties with Greek culture. The inventor Hero lived in Alexandria. So did Dionysius, inventor of the repeating catapult. Another resident was Ctesibius, who lived in the 100s B.C.

Ctesibius was an inventor and a physicist. He studied pneumatics, the science of compressed air. He also studied hydraulics, the science of the force of water and other liquids. He learned how to use both air and water to power machines. His inventions include air pumps, water pumps, and water-driven musical instruments.

Ctesibius also improved on the Egyptian water clock. His clock had a float that sat in a jar of water. A pointer was mounted on top of the float. As water dripped out of a hole in the jar, the float moved downward with the water level. With each unit of passing time, the pointer turned a gear. The turning of the gear caused a pebble to drop, sounded a horn, or made another signal to announce the passage of time. The ancient Roman engineer Marcus Vitruvius, who lived in the first century B.C., wrote this description of Ctesibius's water clock:

> In this [jar], the float . . . is placed beside a drum [gear] that can turn. They are provided with equally spaced teeth, which teeth impinging on [gripping] one another cause suitable turnings and movements . . . by which statues are moved . . . pebbles or eggs are thrown, trumpets sound.

Ctesibius wrote several books about his inventions and discoveries, but none of them survived to modern times. Most of what we know about Ctesibius comes from the works of other ancient writers, such as Vitruvius.

BIGGER, BETTER, AND DEADLIER

Some historians think that catapults were around long before Dionysius the Elder. The Hebrew Bible tells of a king named Uzziah. He lived in Jerusalem, in modern-day Israel, around 800 B.C. To prepare for war, "he made machines designed by skillful men for use on the towers and on the corner defenses to shoot arrows and hurl large stones." Such machines sound a lot like catapults. Whatever the origins of catapults, historians do know that Dionysius used catapults in his war with Carthage.

Ancient Greek catapults had big flexible bows mounted on strong wooden frames. The bows were made of wood, animal horn, and animal tendon. These materials were strong yet flexible. The bowstrings were made of animal tendons, animal hair, and other fibers. Soldiers readied a catapult by turning a crank or a winch. The machine pulled on the bowstring. A trigger mechanism released the bowstring.

Ancient catapults were enormous. One was as tall as a telephone pole. It rested on a base measuring about 8 feet (2.4 m) by 8 feet. Catapults shot arrows and rocks much farther and more accurately than any earlier weapon. Some catapults shot 13-foot (4 m) arrows and 172-pound (78 kg) stones.

"Then at daybreak he [Demetrius; later king of Macedon, near Greece] brought his engines into the harbour with the sound of trumpets and with shouts; and with the lighter catapults, which had a long range, he drove back those who were constructing the wall along the harbour, and with the ballistae [large crossbow] he shook or destroyed the engines of the enemy."

—Diodorus Siculus, Greek historian, first century B.C.

A NEW RELIANCE ON ENGINEERS

In the third century B.C., Greek engineers created a complex formula to design catapults. The formula stated that the diameter (width) of one part of the catapult had to be 1.1 times the cube root of one hundred times the weight of the stone to be hurled. Finding cube roots involves advanced mathematics.

The ancient Greeks could no longer look down on engineers and other craftspeople. They needed skilled mathematicians to design catapults and skilled engineers to build them. The Greek army created an elite team of soldiers to operate catapults. Their work did not involve hand-to-hand fighting. When catapult operators were killed in battle, they could not be replaced by ordinary soldiers.

HIGH TECH

In the 200s B.C., an engineer named Dionysius invented a repeating catapult. Like a repeating rifle, this catapult fired one arrow after another from a firing chamber. A flat-linked chain, similar to a bicycle chain, turned the chamber. As each arrow left the chamber, another arrow fell into position for firing.

▶ This model of a repeating catapult was made in the early 1900s using Greek inventor Dionysius's original plans.

The repeating catapult never replaced single-shot machines, however. For one thing, it had a short range. It could fire an arrow only about 600 feet (183 m). Ordinary catapults could fire arrows 1,815 feet (550 m). Officers also disliked the repeating catapult. They thought it encouraged soldiers to waste ammunition. Although the repeating catapult never caught on, it still represented an important advance in machine technology. It was the first appearance of the flat-linked chain, which is still used in many modern machines.

Another modern tool also debuted in Greek catapults. It was the universal joint. This is a linking device that connects two shafts. Universal joints are found in many modern machines, including cars. The joint got its name because it allows movement in all, or universal, directions. Engineers use universal joints to transmit power when two shafts do not line up exactly. Ancient Greek engineers needed this kind of joint so they could rotate and aim catapults in almost any direction. They created a device very similar to the modern universal joint.

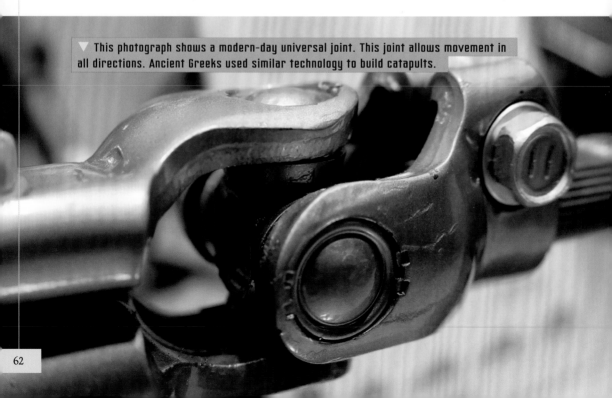

▼ This photograph shows a modern-day universal joint. This joint allows movement in all directions. Ancient Greeks used similar technology to build catapults.

THE WALLS COME TUMBLING DOWN

Ancient cities were usually surrounded by large stone walls. Most of the time, the walls provided protection against enemy invasions. But ancient invaders came up with a clever technique for defeating walled cities. This technique was the siege.

During a siege, an army surrounded an enemy city and repeatedly fired on the city walls. The attacking army also prevented food, water, and fuel from entering the city. People inside the city walls—both soldiers and ordinary citizens—grew cold and hungry. If the siege went on long enough, they began to starve. To relieve their suffering, besieged people often surrendered to their attackers.

Sieges did not always succeed quickly. They often went on for years. According to the legend of the Trojan War (possibly around 1200 B.C.), the Greek siege of the city of Troy lasted for ten years.

With the invention of catapults, sieges became much shorter. An attacking army could aim its catapults at one area of a city's walls. By repeatedly battering one section of wall, attackers could knock it down quickly. In the 200s B.C., a military engineer named Philo of Byzantium (modern-day Istanbul, Turkey) wrote that city walls had to be at least 15 feet (4.6 m) thick to withstand catapult stones.

CHANGING WARFARE

Catapults brought about the first psychological warfare. This tactic involves trying to discourage and frighten enemies rather than just physically attacking them. During sieges, soldiers aimed their catapults during the day. Then they fired them at night to keep city residents awake and on edge. Sometimes, defending soldiers turned and ran at the mere sight of an enemy rolling a catapult into firing position.

Catapults also changed naval warfare. Ancient warships were people powered. Rowers sat one in front of the other along each side of the ship.

Ancient Greek ships called triremes had three banks of rowers on each side, for a total of 170 men pulling on oars.

To attack an enemy ship, the rowers paddled at high speed. They steered their boat right into the side of the opposing ship. They rammed and usually damaged it. Then sailors boarded the enemy ship. Once on board, sailors battled with swords and spears in hand-to-hand combat.

But navies armed with catapults fought long-distance battles. They no longer rammed and boarded enemy ships. And since the ships did not have to reach high speeds for ramming, they needed fewer rowers. Thus warships became smaller. Shipbuilders also began to add layers of armor to protect ships against catapult stones.

EUREKA!

Archimedes was one of the most important mathematicians and engineers of the ancient world. He lived in Greece in the 200s B.C. He is most famous for discovering the principle of buoyancy. This principle explains why objects float, rise, or sink when they are placed in liquid. Legend says that Archimedes discovered the principle while sitting in a bathtub. According to the story, when he came up with his theory, he ran naked into the street yelling, "Eureka!" or "I have found it!"

As a mathematician, Archimedes laid the foundation for calculus. This system of mathematics is used in many branches of engineering. Archimedes discovered the basics of the system, including how to figure the area and the volume of cylinders and spheres. He described many mathematical techniques in a book called *The Method*.

Archimedes also invented machines. The Archimedes screw was a device for pumping water from rivers and irrigation channels. The screw was a hollow shaft with a spiral tube inside. By rotating the shaft with a crank, a person could pump water from the bottom of the tube to the top.

This modern model shows how a person used the Archimedes screw to pump water. As the screw turned, water traveled up the tube and poured out the top.

"I WILL MOVE THE EARTH"

Historians think that Archimedes invented the compound pulley, or block and tackle. A block and tackle is a combination of two different types of pulleys. The pulley at the top of a flagpole is usually a fixed pulley. Fixed pulleys don't increase the force of a person's pull. They simply change the direction of force. They allow a person to pull downward to move a load upward.

Another type of pulley is a movable pulley. In this device, a load is attached to the grooved wheel of the pulley. A rope passes through the groove. One end of the rope is tied to a fixed support above the load (for example, a hook on a ceiling). A person pulls on the other end of the rope to lift the load. A movable pulley has a mechanical advantage of two. It doubles the force of a person's pull.

A block and tackle combines a fixed pulley with movable pulleys. The fixed pulley is attached to a support, such as a strong hook in an overhead beam. This pulley changes the direction of force. A movable pulley is attached to the load. Still other movable pulleys are attached to ropes in between. The mechanical advantage of a compound pulley depends on the number of pulleys. The more pulleys the device has, the greater the mechanical advantage.

Archimedes studied levers and proved a theory called the law of the lever. The law explains how a lever can lift loads of different weights with the same amount of force, depending on the position of the fulcrum. After discovering the law, Archimedes made a famous statement about the power of levers. He said, "Give me a place to stand, and I will move the Earth!"

One story says that the Greek king Hiero of Syracuse heard about Archimedes' boast. Hiero and Archimedes were friends and cousins. Hiero challenged Archimedes to single-handedly launch a huge warship from the dry dock where it had been built. Hiero even had the ship fully loaded with crew and cargo. Such a job would have normally required hundreds of strong men pulling on ropes. But Archimedes did the job single-handedly, as Hiero had asked. Archimedes was probably in his sixties by then. How did he launch the ship alone? He built a system of compound pulleys. They allowed him to move the ship while sitting comfortably in a chair on the dock. All he had to do was pull on a few ropes.

ARCHIMEDES' WAR MACHINES

The ancient Romans tried to capture Syracuse in 214 B.C. The Romans planned to set big covered ladders against the city walls. Then soldiers would swarm over the top of the walls and into Syracuse.

But the Syracuse defenders had prepared well for the attack. At the time, Archimedes was serving as a military adviser to King Hiero. Archimedes designed huge cranes, much like modern construction cranes. Like modern cranes, these machines could swivel around, lift things high in the air, and drop things from great heights. They were rigged with ropes and pulleys and powered by oxen. The cranes could lift huge boulders and lead balls weighing 600 pounds (272 kg). When the Romans approached Syracuse in their ships, operators swung the top of the cranes over the city walls. The cranes dropped boulders and balls on the attacking ships and smashed them.

Soldiers also used a weapon called the Claws of Archimedes to defend Syracuse. This too was a giant crane with ropes and pulleys. One end of the crane had a big clawlike hook hanging from the end of a rope. When the Romans attacked, the Syracuse defenders lowered the hook into the water. The hook snagged the hull of an approaching Roman ship. Then oxen and pulleys went into action. They pulled the rope and lifted the enemy ship right out of the water.

The Greek writer Plutarch (ca. A.D. 46–119) lived several centuries after Archimedes. He wrote about the famous inventor, as well as other

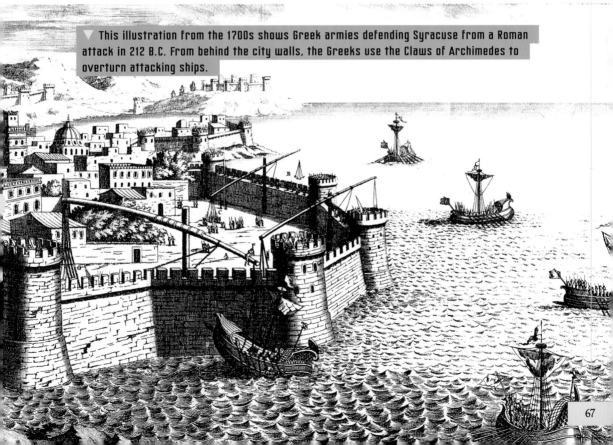

This illustration from the 1700s shows Greek armies defending Syracuse from a Roman attack in 212 B.C. From behind the city walls, the Greeks use the Claws of Archimedes to overturn attacking ships.

acclaimed Greeks and Romans. He gave this description of the Claws of Archimedes:

> The ships, drawn by engines within and whirled about, were
> dashed against steep rocks that stood jutting out under the walls,
> with great destruction of the soldiers that were aboard them. A
> ship was frequently lifted to a great height in the air (a dreadful
> thing to behold) and was rolled to and fro, and kept swinging,
> until the mariners [sailors] were all thrown out, when at length it
> was dashed against the rocks, or was let fall.

GEARS

Gears are machines that transfer motion from one turning shaft to another turning shaft. The first gears were wooden wheels with small spokes projecting from the rim. These spokes meshed (fit together) with spokes in another wheel. The motion of the first wheel turned the second wheel.

No one knows who made the first gears, but they were widely used in ancient times. Ancient Greek engineers were fascinated with gears. They learned that gears could do more than just transfer motion. They could also change the direction, force, and speed of motion. For example, a small gear turning a larger gear increases force. A large gear turning a smaller gear increases speed. Gears can also be combined into gear trains to achieve various combinations of speed, force, and direction.

The world's first known description of gears and gear trains comes from a book named *Mechanica.* Written in the 300s or 200s B.C., it is the oldest known engineering textbook. Some experts think the Greek scientist and philosopher Aristotle wrote *Mechanica.* Others think a Greek engineer named Strato of Lampsacus was the author. In addition to describing gears, *Mechanica* includes a discussion of friction.

THE ANTIKYTHERA MECHANISM

One day in 1900, divers were searching the seafloor near the Greek island of Antikythera. They were looking for natural sponges, but they discovered the wreck of an ancient cargo ship instead. It had sunk about two thousand years earlier. The divers brought up many relics, or remains, from the shipwreck. These included marble statues and pieces of bronze.

As archaeologists cleaned the bronze, they discovered a series of gears *(see the one shown above)*. The gears were precisely made. They were obviously the remains of a machine. What was it?

In the 1950s, British historian Derek de Solla Price began studying the machine. After years of work, he concluded that it was an astronomical calendar from ancient Greece. The device had more than thirty gears. It calculated the movements of the sun, the moon, and the planets.

De Solla Price built a model based on the ancient gears. He found that the machine looked much like an old-fashioned table clock. It had probably been housed inside a wooden case with a door.

In 2006 scientists took a closer look at the Antikythera Mechanism. Using three-dimensional X-ray scanners and other imaging machines, they were able to learn even more about the bronze gears. They found inscriptions on the gears that had not been seen before. They found that the machine contained several calendars, including solar (sun-based) and lunar (moon-based) calendars. They determined that the machine was built between 150 and 100 B.C. The new research showed that the machine was even more advanced than scientists had first realized. It could predict solar and lunar eclipses (the obscuring of the sun or the moon when another celestial body passes in front of it). It could even track the irregular motions of the moon around Earth.

CHAPTER SEVEN

ANCIENT ROME

▲ The Pont du Gard is an aqueduct (water-carrying channel) built by the ancient Romans in the A.D. 100s in southern France.

The ancient Romans loved machines. Roman engineers used mechanical knowledge to build roads, bridges, aqueducts, mills, and weapons. Greek mathematicians developed geometry and trigonometry. But the Greeks mostly admired these systems for the sheer love of knowledge. Roman engineers put these systems to practical use in construction projects. Little of what Roman engineers did was original. But the Romans did a good job of improving on technology developed by other ancient cultures.

A NEW PRIME MOVER

A prime mover is a machine that transforms heat, wind, or flowing water into mechanical energy that can power other machines. A prime mover might rotate a shaft, which then turns a wheel or a gear. Prime movers include waterwheels, windmills, steam engines, internal combustion engines, and jet engines.

Human muscles were the first prime movers. Animals were the next prime movers. When placed in harnesses, animals could turn larger mills and carry heavier loads than humans could. Oxen were especially important to ancient peoples. These large animals are extremely strong.

It took about seven thousand years for people to develop the next prime mover. This was the waterwheel.

▲ In this stone carving, a donkey pushes a lever to turn an ancient Roman grain mill.

PEOPLE OR MACHINES?

Ancient Romans loved machines. But they had one of the same concerns about technology that modern people have. Technology sometimes increases unemployment. Modern factories that use robots need fewer employees than factories that rely on people power for the same job.

Emperors in ancient Rome wanted to keep people at their jobs rather than replacing them with machines. Suetonius, a Roman historian who lived from about A.D. 69 to 122, told this story about Roman emperor Vespasian:

> An engineer offered to haul some huge columns up to the Capitol [a building] at moderate expense by a simple mechanical contrivance [machine], but Vespasian declined his services: "I must always ensure," he said, "that the working classes earn enough money to buy themselves food."

THE GREEK MILL

Early peoples used waterwheels primarily to grind grain. Ancient Greeks made the first waterwheel in the first century B.C. It was a wooden wheel with six to eight scoops connected to a central shaft. The wheel sat horizontally in a fast-running stream. Water pushed on the scoops and turned the wheel. The central shaft also turned. The turning shaft worked a series of gears, which in turn powered millstones. The moving stones crushed grain into flour. The ancient Greek mill was not very powerful. It took several hours to grind 100 pounds (45 kg) of grain.

THE ROMAN MILL

Roman engineers copied the Greek mill and greatly improved its design. They converted the horizontal waterwheel into a vertical (upright) waterwheel.

The Romans made two kinds of vertical waterwheels. The undershot wheel had blades that dipped into moving water. As the current pushed the blades, the wheel turned. More efficient was the overshot wheel. It used a chute (a type of slide) to pour water over the top of the wheel. Both the current of the river and the weight of the falling water turned the wheel. Water weighs a lot—about 8 pounds (3.6 kg) per gallon. The extra weight of the falling water made the overshot wheel turn faster than the undershot wheel.

The ancient Roman mill was a powerful new prime mover. Experts estimate that even the most primitive Roman mill could grind thousands of pounds of grain a day.

The Roman mill is sometimes called the Vitruvian mill. It was named for its inventor, Marcus Vitruvius. The Vitruvian mill gave Romans the most powerful prime mover in the ancient world. Yet the ancient Romans never used the mill on a wide scale. Of the three hundred grain mills in the city of Rome during the A.D. 200s, only a few were powered by water. Most were powered by slaves.

Why not use water power instead? Some experts think the ancient Romans saw no

▲ This page from Marcus Vitruvius's *On Architecture* written around 25 B.C., shows his design for a water-powered grain mill.

> "Wheels on rivers are constructed upon the same principles as those just described. Round their circumference [outer rims] are fixed paddles, which, when acted upon by the force of the current, drive the wheel round, receive the water in the buckets, and carry it to the top."

—Marcus Vitruvius, *On Architecture*, first century B.C.

need for mechanized mills. They had plenty of slaves for cheap labor. People rarely take advantage of technology unless they need it or see its benefits.

AN ANCIENT FACTORY

France was once part of the vast Roman Empire. In a place called Barbegal, France, archaeologists have found the remains of sixteen stone buildings with waterwheels. Archaeologists think the site was an immense factory for milling grain. It was built in the A.D. 300s. An inscription on a nearby tomb suggests that the mill was built by Quintus Candidius Benignus, a Roman engineer. The inscription praises him for being "clever like none other, and none surpassed him in the construction of machines."

The stone buildings stood in two parallel rows of eight buildings each. Both rows ran down the slope of a hill. Each building contained its own waterwheel. Two channels of water ran down the hill, cascading onto the first wheel, then the next, and then the next. After turning the final wheel, the water ran into a drain and out to a marshy area about 0.25 mile (0.4 km) away.

Archaeologists estimate that the sixteen waterwheels produced enough power to grind about 9,900 pounds (4,491 kg) of flour each day. That flour could have fed about 12,500 people. The mill probably produced flour for the nearby city of Arles, which had a population of about 12,000 at the time.

The ancient factory probably produced no more than 30 horsepower. That's equal to about six modern self-propelled

▲ In the A.D. 300s, water ran downhill and turned waterwheels in sixteen stone buildings here in Barbegal, France. In modern times, only some of the ancient stones remain.

lawn mowers. But experts believe that it had the greatest concentration of mechanical power in ancient Europe.

GOING UP

The ancient Romans were famous for moving water. They built a series of aqueducts to carry water from mountain springs into big cities. Most aqueducts were elevated structures. They looked like bridges running over

Ctesibius of Alexandria invented a water pump in the 200s B.C. This device consisted of two parallel bronze cylinders. Inside the cylinders were movable valves called pistons. When a person moved the pump handle, one piston sucked water up into the first cylinder while the other piston pushed the water down through the second cylinder. From the second cylinder, the water ran into a tank or a nozzle. This type of pump is called a force pump. The ancient Romans improved on Ctesibius's force pump. They created big force pumps to fight fires, drain water from ships, and bring drinking water up from wells.

both land and water. The aqueducts sloped slightly downward. The downward slope allowed gravity to pull water down through the channels to cities.

Sometimes, however, the Romans and other ancient peoples needed to move water up, not down. They needed to raise water from wells or into elevated storage tanks. For this job, ancient peoples built enormous water-lifting devices. One part of the device sat in a river or a well. It contained big buckets for scooping up water.

▼ A modern-day model shows how the Roman water-lifting wheel, called a *noria*, worked. Jugs attached to the wheel scooped up water from the bottom and emptied them into chutes or irrigation channels as they rounded the top.

Next to the water source, people or animals turned a giant shaft. The shaft was connected to a series of gears. The turning gears moved a chain, which moved the buckets. When a bucket reached its highest level, its water drained out into an irrigation channel or a storage tank.

In addition to lifting water for drinking and farming, the ancient Romans used water-lifting machines to supply water to their public baths. These gathering places were like modern-day spas. Romans bathed, swam, took saunas, exercised, and socialized there. The water for the facilities was stored in overhead cisterns, or tanks. It had to be carried up several stories with water-lifting machines.

▼ The ancient Romans used water-lifting machines to carry water to public baths, such as this one in Herculaneum in western Italy. The town was destroyed by the eruption of Mount Vesuvius in A.D. 79.

AFTER THE ANCIENTS

Ancient societies rose and fell. Often groups grew politically or economically weak and stronger groups conquered them. But even after a society fell, its technology often remained. Conquering groups built on the knowledge of conquered peoples to further develop technology.

This wasn't always the case, however. After the Roman Empire fell to invaders in A.D. 476, Europe entered a period called the Middle Ages (about 500 to 1500). The early Middle Ages are sometimes called the Dark Ages because art, culture, and learning were minimal in Europe during these years. Few people in Europe went to school. Few craftspeople knew about or improved upon ancient technology.

REWRITTEN

Many ancient libraries were neglected during the Middle Ages. Some libraries burned to the ground. Others were destroyed in war. In this way, many writings about ancient technology disappeared.

But even when ancient libraries survived, manuscripts were still lost. In ancient times, people wrote on parchment, which is made from animal skins. In the Middle Ages, when scribes (trained writers) wanted to write new manuscripts, they sometimes scraped the text off old manuscripts. They washed the parchment clean and wrote new text over the old words. Scribes reused old parchment in part to save money, since parchment was expensive. In many cases, scribes didn't care about the old documents they scraped away. They often wrote religious texts on the newly washed parchment, because religion was central to European life in the Middle Ages.

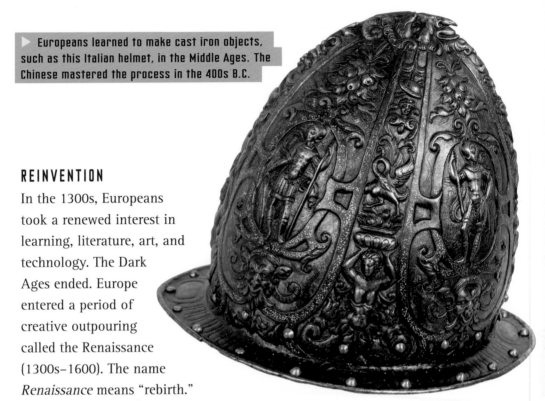

REINVENTION

In the 1300s, Europeans took a renewed interest in learning, literature, art, and technology. The Dark Ages ended. Europe entered a period of creative outpouring called the Renaissance (1300s–1600). The name *Renaissance* means "rebirth."

During the Renaissance, Europeans found many ancient manuscripts, such as Marcus Vitruvius's *On Architecture*. As they researched ancient cultures, European peoples learned about machines and other technology from ancient Egypt, Greece, Rome, the Middle East, and China.

At the same time, Europeans invented new machines. In many cases, craftspeople reinvented machines and technology that ancient peoples had already created more than one thousand years before. For instance, people in Europe learned to cast iron in the early 1300s. But they were hundreds of years behind the ancient Chinese, who had invented the technique in the 400s B.C. In the 1400s, Italian artist and inventor Leonardo da Vinci designed a flat-linked chain. He didn't know that Dionysius had used a similar flat-linked chain on his repeating catapult in the 300s B.C. In the 1500s, Italian mathematician Geronimo Cardano designed a universal joint. This too was a reinvention. The ancient Greeks had already used universal joints on catapults. In 1698 English military engineer Thomas Savery devised a steam engine. People thought it was a brand-new machine. They didn't know that Hero had created a steam engine more than sixteen hundred years earlier in Alexandria.

REVOLUTION

In the mid-1700s, Europe entered an era known as the Industrial Revolution. This revolution changed Europe from a farming society to a society based on large-scale manufacturing. Many people moved from farms to cities during this time. In the cities, manufacturers opened large factories. There, people ran power-driven machines. Factories could produce goods more quickly, more cheaply, and in greater quantities than craftspeople could by hand.

During the Industrial Revolution, people made machines that surpassed the inventions of ancient Greece and other ancient societies. In 1769 Scottish engineer James Watt perfected the steam engine. His engine could power machines, ships, and trains. Other engineers perfected pumps and differential gears during this era. They put these devices to practical use in factories and vehicles.

▼ During the Industrial Revolution, people began to build machines that surpassed those of ancient times. James Watt's steam engine, on display at a German museum, is one example.

REDISCOVERY

Meanwhile, inventors continued to build on the wisdom of ancient machine makers. People continued to discover ancient texts. In 1899 a Greek scholar cataloged some ancient religious manuscripts stored in Constantinople (modern-day Istanbul), Turkey. He noticed that one of the manuscripts had some ancient Greek "undertext" beneath the religious writing. This text had been scraped off and written over in the early 1200s. But it was still visible. The scholar translated a few lines of undertext. He contacted another scholar, who was an expert on ancient Greece. That scholar realized that the undertext was written by Archimedes. The ancient parchment contained three of Archimedes' books, including *The Method*. This discovery was a major breakthrough for scholars. Archimedes' books provided brand-new information about ancient technology.

RECONSTRUCTION

Engineers around the world became fascinated by ancient machines. In the early 1900s, Erwin Schramm, a German military officer, reconstructed ancient catapults using original plans created by Dionysius's engineers. Schramm found these devices to be extremely accurate. In one demonstration, catapult operators fired an arrow into a target and then fired another arrow that split the first one in two.

Later in the twentieth century, engineers built steam engines based on Hero's design. They found that Hero's engine had rotated up to fifteen hundred times per minute. Modern engineers have also reconstructed the Chinese south-pointing carriage, Greek warships, Roman mills, the Antikythera Mechanism, and other ancient machines.

Sometimes museums display the remains of ancient machines alongside modern reconstructions. Some museums even let visitors operate the reconstructed machines. For instance, in 2002 the Museum of London in England built a full-size model of a two-thousand-year-old

Places such as the Museum of London show visitors ancient technology firsthand. People can push big wooden bars to operate this re-creation of a Roman-era water-lifting machine.

Roman water-lifting machine. The replica was based on the remains of two real machines used in London, England, when England was part of the Roman Empire. Modern visitors can push big wooden bars to turn the giant shaft that operates the machine. In ancient times, slaves probably did the pushing. Engineers say that the machine would have been able to lift 15,000 gallons (56,800 liters) of water each day.

REUSE

The word *ancient* sometimes means "old-fashioned," or "out of date." It's true that many ancient machines seem poorly suited to the modern world. After all, why travel by oxcart when you can take a car, a bus, a subway, or an airplane?

But on closer examination, many "ancient" machines aren't so out of fashion after all. Look at the website or mail-order catalog of a popular cooking store such as Williams-Sonoma or Crate and Barrel. These shops sell mortars and pestles that look very much like mortars and pestles found in ancient Jordan and dating to 12,500 B.C.

Does your family have a wheelbarrow in the garage or backyard? It probably looks a lot like the "wooden ox" and "gliding horse" built in ancient China in the first century A.D. Although your wheelbarrow might be made from stronger and lighter materials, it combines the same two simple machines and operates on the exact same principles as the old Chinese wheelbarrow.

Have you ever gone tobogganing in winter? Perhaps you used a plastic toboggan. But one company in Minnesota specializes in building "traditional handmade sleighs in the Algonkian and Athapaskin [Indian] tradition." The toboggans are made out of thick pieces of oak, with curved fronts that glide smoothly across the snow. The design is nearly identical to that used by ancient Native Americans. The company believes that ancient Americans had devised the best technology for traveling over the snow—and it doesn't want to mess with a good thing. Hundreds and even thousands of years after ancient times, people still can't improve on some ancient machines.

TIMELINE

CA. 14,000 B.C.	People in ancient Japan begin to make pottery.
CA. 10,000 B.C.	People in the ancient Middle East begin farming.
CA. 6000 B.C.	People in eastern Europe invent the loom.
CA. 3500 B.C.	People in Mesopotamia create the first wheeled vehicles. People in Mesopotamia create the potter's wheel.
CA. 2600 B.C.	Egyptians build the Great Pyramid.
CA. 1500 B.C.	Ancient Egyptians build the clepsydra, or water clock.
CA. 1200 B.C.	The Hittites smelt iron to create iron tools and weapons.
CA. 1000 B.C.	People in Peru learn to make bronze.
CA. 400 B.C.	The Chinese learn to cast iron.
390S B.C.	Dionysius the Elder uses catapults in a war against Carthage.
300S B.C.	People in China invent crossbows.
200S B.C.	The Chinese invent the bellows. The engineer Dionysius invents a repeating catapult. Archimedes invents machines and writes books on engineering, physics, and mathematics.
CA. 100 B.C.	People in ancient Greece make the first waterwheel.
CA. 1ST CENTURY A.D.	Hero of Alexandria invents machines and writes books on mathematics, physics, and mechanics.
A.D. 30	Chinese official Tu Shih invents a water-powered bellows.
132	Chinese scientist Chang Heng builds a seismograph.
CA. 300S	Ancient Romans build a milling factory at Barbegal, France.
476	The Roman Empire falls to invaders.
500	Europe enters the Middle Ages.
1300	Europe enters the Renaissance.
1700S	The Industrial Revolution begins in Europe.

1899	Greek scholars discover an ancient manuscript containing Archimedes' *The Method* and other books.
1900	Greek divers discover the Antikythera Mechanism in the sea near a Greek island.
EARLY 1900S	Erwin Schramm reconstructs ancient Greek catapults.
1950S	History professor Derek de Solla Price begins to study the Antikythera Mechanism.
2002	The Museum of London in England constructs a full-size replica of a Roman water-lifting machine.
2006	Archaeologists learn new details about the Antikythera Mechanism.

GLOSSARY

ARCHAEOLOGIST: a scientist who studies the remains of past cultures

ARTIFACT: a human-made object, especially one characteristic of a certain group or historical period

CAST: to create objects by pouring melted metal into molds and letting it harden

ENGINEER: a person who designs and builds machines, structures, and other objects

FORCE: physical effort that causes an object to move or stop moving

FRICTION: the force that slows motion when one surface rubs against another

FULCRUM: the pivot point around which a lever turns in raising or moving an object

GEAR: a toothed wheel that transfers motion and power from one part of a machine to another

HUNTER-GATHERERS: people who get their food by hunting wild animals and gathering roots, fruits, and other plants

INCLINED PLANE: a ramp or other angled surface that reduces the force needed to lift objects

IRRIGATE: to supply water to farmland using channels, reservoirs, pumps, and other machines

LEVER: a bar used to lift or move objects. A person applies force to one end of the bar to lift or move a load on the other end. The bar pivots on a support called a fulcrum.

MACHINE: a device that does work by increasing or changing the direction of force

MECHANICAL ADVANTAGE: the degree to which a machine increases force

PRIME MOVER: a machine that provides energy to power another machine

PULLEY: a grooved wheel attached to a rope. Pulleys change the direction of force.

SCREW: a rod surrounded by a spiral ridge that works like an inclined plane. People use screws to fasten and lift objects.

SIMPLE MACHINES: six machines that form the basis for all other machines. The simple machines are the lever, the wheel and axle, the pulley, the inclined plane, the wedge, and the screw.

SMELT: to separate metal from ore by heating it in a furnace

WEDGE: a tool that is thicker at one end than at the other. Wedges move objects short distances.

WHEEL AND AXLE: a combination of two wheels of different sizes. The wheel and axle increases or reduces force.

WORK: the amount of energy needed to move an object over a particular distance

35 L. Cranmer-Byng and S. A. Kapadia, eds. *The Instruction of Ptah-Hotep*, Battiscombe Gunn trans. (London: John Murray, 1912), 70.

36 L. Sprague de Camp, *The Ancient Engineers* (Garden City, NY: Doubleday, 1963), 30.

42 Hong-Sen Yan, *Reconstruction Designs of Lost Ancient Chinese Machinery* (Dordrecht, Netherlands: Springer, 2007), 275.

45 UNESCO Courier, "A Cybernet Machine," BNET, October 1988, http://findarticles.com/p/articles/mi_m1310/is_1988_Oct/ai_6955862/ (May 15, 2010).

46 Peter James and Nick Thorpe, *Ancient Inventions* (New York: Ballentine, 1994), 143.

50 Bernal Diaz Del Castillo, *The Memoirs of the Conquistador Bernal Diaz del Castillo*, vol. 1 (London: J. Hatchard and Son, 1844), 231.

59 Donald Hill, *A History of Engineering in Classical and Medieval Times* (London: Routledge, 1996), 227.

60 2 Chronicles 26:13–15 (New International Version).

60 Diodorus Siculus, "The Library of History," Bill Thayer, November 30, 2008, http://penelope.uchicago.edu/Thayer/E/Roman/Texts/Diodorus_Siculus/20D*.html (May 14, 2010).

66 Stone, *Routledge Dictionary*, 241.

68 Plutarch, "Plutarch's Lives," Project Gutenberg, October 1996, http://www.gutenberg.org/dirs/etext96/plivs10.txt (May 14, 2010).

72 Colin Chant and David C. Goodman, *Pre-industrial Cities and Technology* (London: Routledge, 1999), 98.

74 Marcus Vitruvius Pollio, "De Architectura, Book X," Bill Thayer, November 30, 2008, http://penelope.uchicago.edu/Thayer/E/Roman/Texts/Vitruvius/10*.html (May 14, 2010).

74 Robert James Forbes, *Studies in Ancient Technology*, vol. 2 (Leiden, Netherlands: E. J. Brill, 1993), 95.

83 Northern Toboggan and Sled, "Supplier of Traditional Towing Toboggans and Freight Sleds for the Canadian North," Northern Toboggan and Sled, 2008, http://www.ntsled.com/ (May 14, 2010).

SELECTED BIBLIOGRAPHY

Bruno, Leonard C. *The Tradition of Technology: Landmarks of Western Technology.* Washington, DC: Library of Congress, 1995.

Bunch, Bryan, and Alexander Hellemans. *The Timetables of Technology.* New York: Simon & Schuster, 1993.

Diamond, Jared. *Guns, Germs, and Steel: The Fates of Human Societies.* Rev. ed. New York: W. W. Norton, 2005.

Fagen, Brian, ed. *Discovery! Unearthing the New Treasures of Archaeology.* London: Thames and Hudson, 2007.

———. *The Seventy Great Inventions of the Ancient World.* London: Thames and Hudson, 2004.

Hackett, John. *Warfare in the Ancient World.* New York: Facts on File, 1989.

Hill, Donald. *A History of Engineering in Classical and Medieval Times.* London: Routledge, 1996.

Scarre, Chris. *Smithsonian Timelines of the Ancient World: A Visual Chronology from the Origins of Life to A.D. 1500.* London: Dorling Kindersley, 1993.

Schick, Kathy D., and Nicholas Toth. *Making Silent Stones Speak: Human Evolution and the Dawn of Technology.* New York: Simon & Schuster, 1993.

Schiller, Ronald. *Distant Secrets: Unraveling the Mysteries of Our Ancient Past.* New York: Carol Publishing, 1989.

Soedel, Werner, and Vernard Foley. "Ancient Catapults." *Scientific American,* March 1979, 150–160.

Williams, Trevor I. *The History of Invention.* New York: Facts on File, 1987.

FURTHER READING

DK Publishing, *Early Humans*. New York: DK Children, 2005. Early humans
    made simple machines for hunting, travel, and food preparation.
    Illustrated with full-color photos, this book examines the lives of the
    first peoples on Earth.

Opik, E. J. *Ancient China*. New York: DK Children, 2005. This beautifully
    illustrated title offers a wealth of information on ancient Chinese
    technology, art, and culture.

Passport to History series. Minneapolis: Twenty-First Century Books, 2001–
    2004. In this series, readers will take trips back in time to ancient China,
    Egypt, Greece, Rome, and the Mayan civilization. They will learn about
    people's clothing, work, tools, and other aspects of daily life.

Rice, Rob S. *Ancient Greek Warfare*. New York: Gareth Stevens Publishing,
    2009. The ancient Greeks fought battles on both land and sea. This book
    looks at Greek weapons, such as catapults, and tactics, such as sieges.

Schomp, Virginia. *Ancient Mesopotamia: The Sumerians, Babylonians, and
    Assyrians*. Danbury, CT: Children's Press, 2005. Mesopotamians invented
    one of the most important machines of all times—the wheel. Read
    about the cultures of ancient Mesopotamia and their contributions to
    technology.

Unearthing Ancient Worlds series. Minneapolis: Twenty-First Century
    Books, 2008–2009. This series takes readers on journeys of discovery, as
    archaeologists discover King Tut's tomb, the royal Incan city of Machu
    Picchu, the ruins of Pompeii, and other archaeological treasures.

Visual Geography Series. Minneapolis: Twenty-First Century Books,
    2003–2011. Each book in this series examines one country, with lots of
    information about its ancient history. The series' companion website—
    vgsbooks.com—offers free, downloadable material and links to sites with
    additional information about each country.

Woods, Michael, and Mary B. Woods. Seven Wonders of the Ancient
World series. Minneapolis: Twenty-First Century Books, 2009. This
series explores Herodotus's list of the seven ancient wonders as well
as magnificent buildings and monuments from ancient Africa, Asia,
Central and South America, and North America.

Zannos, Susan. *The Life and Times of Archimedes.* Hockessin, DE: Mitchell
Lane Publishers, 2004. Archimedes invented machines and studied
physics and mathematics. This book describes his life and the world in
which he worked.

WEBSITES

EGYPT: SECRETS OF THE ANCIENT WORLD
http://www.nationalgeographic.com/pyramids/
Created by *National Geographic* magazine, this website offers interactive
features, fun and games, and up-to-date news about the pyramids and
other wonders of ancient Egypt.

EXPLORE
http://www.britishmuseum.org/explore/explore_introduction.aspx
This Web page from the British Museum in London, England, opens the
door to ancient cultures, including the Aztecs, Chinese, and others.

http://www.msichicago.org/online-science/simple-machines/activities/
simple-machines-1/

This Web page from the Museum of Science and Industry in Chicago,
Illinois, uses games and animation to introduce the six simple machines.

INDEX

ABOUT THE AUTHORS

Michael Woods is a science and medical journalist in Washington, D.C. He has won many national writing awards. Mary B. Woods is a school librarian. Their past books include the fifteen-volume Disasters Up Close series, the seven-volume Seven Wonders of the Ancient World series, and the seven-volume Seven Wonders of the Natural World series. The Woodses have four children. When not writing, reading, or enjoying their grandchildren, the Woodses travel to gather material for future books.

PHOTO ACKNOWLEDGMENTS